DATE DUE		
~~Aug 15 '73~~ Apr 25 '83		
~~Jul 31 '74~~		
~~Aug 8 '74~~		
~~Aug 14 '74~~		
Oct 28 '75		
May 16 '77		
Dec 13 '77		
May 22 78		
Mar 12 '80		
Dec 10 '82		
Feb 13 '83		
Mar 14 '83		

TWO VIEWS OF A PRISON

The Time Game

Anthony J. Manocchio
and
Jimmy Dunn

WITH AN INTRODUCTION AND POSTSCRIPT BY

LaMar T. Empey

Beverly Hills, California

TWO VIEWS OF A PRISON

The Time Game

 SAGE Publications

365. 019
M31π
77/21
Dec.1971

For information address:

SAGE PUBLICATIONS, INC.
275 South Beverly Drive
Beverly Hills, California 90212

International Standard Book Number 0-8039-0079-1

Library of Congress Catalog Card No. 72-127990

FIRST PRINTING

Contents

Introduction   The Players and the Setting: 9
                  LaMar T. Empey

CHAPTER 1.   Life in Prison: Dunn   29
                  Life at Prison: Murray   43

         2.   The Con: Dunn   57
                  The Interview: Murray   65

         3.   The Red Tape: Dunn   73
                  The Policy-Makers: Murray   83

CHAPTER 4.   The Story Hour: Dunn   109
              The Group Meeting: Murray   119

         5.   The Good Time: Dunn   135
              The Recreation Syndrome: Murray   143

         6.   The Bad Time: Dunn   157
              The Tensions: Murray   161

         7.   A Rehash: Dunn   171
              A Victory of Sorts: Murray   181

         8.   The Goodies: Dunn   185
              The Dependency Syndrome: Murray   193

         9.   The Ordeal: Dunn   207
              The Challenge: Murray   215

        10.   The Parole: Murray   225
              The Cut-Loose: Dunn   231

        11.   Implications: A Game with No Winners   241
              LaMar T. Empey

Postscript   What Happened to Jimmy Dunn?   253
              LaMar T. Empey

References   265

TWO VIEWS OF A PRISON

The Time Game

Introduction

The Players and the Setting

LaMAR T. EMPEY:

In his introduction to a recent edition of Clifford Shaw's *The Jack-Roller* (1966: v-xviii), Howard Becker provides an excellent review of both the virtues and limitations of the sociological life history as a source of social science "data." In the "Golden Age" of Chicago sociology, he notes, the life history was joined with ecological, interview, and other empirical studies to provide a mosaic of findings which has never since been replicated. "Given the variety of scientific uses to which the life history may be put," he says, "one must wonder at the relative neglect into which it has fallen" (1966: xvi). In our current emphasis upon abstract theory-building and the empirical side of social investigation, we have greatly missed the contribution which the life history has to make.

The design and conduct of many, perhaps most, sociological studies depend upon some knowledge of the subjective views of the actors to be investigated. Without it, the investigation must proceed more by assumption than by evidence, more by conjecture than by an informed point of view. To be able to ask relevant questions and to explore key issues, the sociologist must have some prior grasp of the way those issues look to the persons who are to be studied, what they contend with, and why they believe as they do. There is nothing quite so difficult as attempting to gather data on the nature and subjective side of institutional patterns and processes without such information. The life history, by virtue of its wealth of detail, can suggest important research questions, processes to be studied, and variables to be isolated, especially when some area of investigation has grown stagnant, when repeated studies seem to reach an impasse.

To some degree there is such an impasse in the existing literature on the nature of prison life. And it is with respect to this impasse that this book has a contribution to make. Technically, the book is not a life-history document. Rather it is a description of a series of prison experiences as seen from the polar positions of an habitual criminal— Jimmy Dunn—and a prison counselor—Charles Murray. Both Dunn and Murray are real people, describing real events. They were residents in the same prison and not only knew each other, but were the main protagonists in the drama that is portrayed here.

The reader will be interested in how this book came to be written. The events that are described in it occurred when Dunn, the criminal, was in his mid-twenties. Later, at age thirty-two, after he had spent more time in more prisons, he and Murray met again. By then, Murray had left the prison and was working in the community on an experiment being conducted by this writer. Inconsistent with his prior history, Dunn had come to Murray looking for a job. Murray approached me, and I agreed to hire Dunn.

Shortly thereafter, Dunn and Murray came up with the idea for this book. They agreed to describe, from their own perspectives and feelings, the events that are portrayed in later chapters. After they had completed the manuscript, they showed it to me. I had mixed feelings.

On one hand, the events they described were sometimes brutal, sometimes poignant, but always illustrative of a setting in which most of the actors were participants in a game characterized more by manipulation, deceit, and hopelessness than by any adherence to the officially stated objectives of rehabilitation and community protection. Even though my background and interest in corrections did provide me with an intellectual framework for understanding what I read, it did not prepare me in a personal way. It was hard for me to believe that these two close associates could have been such bitter opponents—that they could have seen things from such totally different perspectives. The message was such that I felt it was important for others to receive. It was clear to me that, although they were now friends, they could never have been anything other than distrustful, manipulative, and, so far as Dunn was concerned, even bitter opponents, so long as they remained in the prison system.

On the other hand, the manuscript needed a lot of work. Neither man was an experienced writer, and much editing and reorganizing was necessary. Thus, in the press of our other work, the story lay fallow for nearly five years. Then, in the light of new circumstances (to be described in the postscript of this book), especially as it relates to Dunn and his tenuous survival in the community, the importance of telling the story reasserted itself. The manuscript was revived and prepared for publication. Hopefully, after reading about the experiences of Dunn and Murray in the prison, the reader will become involved, as I was involved, in what eventually happened to Dunn.

Before going into their descriptions of prison life, however, let us pay brief attention to the life histories of Dunn and Murray, and the way these histories are likely to affect their perceptions of the prison. Let us pay attention further to the way in which the dialogue reflects upon the nature of prison organization itself. Our eventual understanding of prison life will depend upon the extent to which we grasp the interactive effects of personal and organizational factors.

JIMMY DUNN

It would be useful if Jimmy could be neatly typed as a particular criminal type. His reactions to prison life, as a result, might be more easily understood and categorized. But that cannot be done. Under some conditions, Dunn has all the marks of what Schrag (1961: 347-348) calls a "right guy," or, more specifically, what Irwin and Cressey (1964) refer to as a "thief"—a career offender who views incarceration as an occupational hazard; who subscribes to the notion that inmates should not betray each other, should be reliable, wily, and coolheaded; and who, because of his sophistication, is able to "do time" with the least possible suffering. As evidence of this categorization, the reader will note that Dunn seldom gets himself on official "report," stays clear of most of the prison rackets, except where he can benefit without danger to himself, knows where he can turn for information when he needs it, and, except for a handful of friends, is contemptuous of almost all other prisoners, whom he calls "hoosiers."

Under other circumstances, however, Dunn has many of the earmarks of a "convict" (compare with Irwin and Cressey, 1964)—a person who has been raised by the state and for whom institutional confinement has become a way of life. The circumstantial evidence in favor of this categorization is overwhelming. Dunn spent fourteen of his nineteen years between the ages of thirteen and thirty-two in confinement. His longest single period of freedom in all that time was only six months and five days. Perhaps that is why, if one reads between the lines, Dunn seems to treat incarceration much like other people treat a confining occupation. He describes prison as a place where he builds himself up physically (he lifts weights), regains his health, as it were, and then when he is released (completes his job) he goes on a terrific binge, using narcotics, running whores, cashing fraudulent checks, burglarizing, and doing other things that result in his being returned to prison. He is like the old-time cowboy, or a construction worker who works seven days a week for several months, isolated from people, and then when he finally gets to town, blows his whole income on a drunken spree. When it is over, he returns, half-sick and penniless, to the job. But, again, there are contradicting signs. Despite the fact that Dunn never finished high school, he is obviously intelligent, literate, and personally attractive. He has a degree of ability and assurance that does not square somehow with the semiliterate and dependent people that one often finds among those who have spent years in total institutions.

In fact, for those who favor a more traditional, psychological interpretation, Dunn could be described as a "psychopath" or "sociopath." He is a skilled manipulator, forms few close personal ties, and has few qualms about using other people, especially women. From the age of fifteen, he emulated his father and became a pimp. He lived off women. Even when he married a young college girl, whom he had recruited for the profession, he expected her to continue her "work" so she could support him: providing narcotics and a livelihood when Dunn was out of prison, furnishing sexual favors to one of his parole officers as a means of compromising the officer, and providing Dunn with spending money when he was locked up. The exploitive character of this latter relationship is clearly spelled out in the narration which follows.

Dunn also organized check-cashing rings, never passing any fraudulent checks himself, but allowing others to run the risks. Still, with all his apparent departure from conventionality, he was not without a sense of ethics and obligation. It was demonstrated at an early age. The first time he was committed to a training school, he was nearly beaten to death by a group of older inmates to whom he refused to bow. Yet, even as he lay in the hospital, seriously hurt, he would not tell on them. From that time, until we read about him here, his loyalty to the *ideals* of the inmate code was undiminished—a loyalty based more upon principle than upon particular friendships.

Despite his obvious intelligence, his concern for self, and his contempt for most inmates, as inmates, Dunn was highly vulnerable if approached by one of his peers for a favor, either in or out of prison. He felt constrained by a compelling sense of obligation. In one of the incidents described in this book, for example, his loyalty extended so far that on the very day of his release from prison, he risked losing all by agreeing to smuggle dope to some acquaintances in the prison. He knew it was foolish, but he could not say no. Thus, while Dunn was scarcely a conformist in a conventional sense, he was not without a sense of obligation to others. The key to understanding his behavior, therefore, lies more in understanding the particular norms and reference groups to which he adhered, rather than assuming that he had none.

His behavior and outlook, as a matter of fact, are testimony to the lasting effects of the kind of socialization he experienced. It helps to explain why, in some circumstances, he appears to be a sophisticated "thief," and why in others, he seems dependent upon an institutional environment.

Dunn's parents separated when he was two and he went to live with an aunt and uncle who were not anxious to have him. When he was six, his mother appeared suddenly, picked him up off the street and took him to live with her. It was as though she had a premonition of what was to follow, and wanted some time with her boy. Within three weeks she was dead (and Jimmy was alone).

Because the six-year-old Jimmy had left his aunt and uncle to live with his mother, they would not take him back. Ultimately, however, his father reluctantly agreed to care for him. Thus, until he was nine, Dunn lived with his bellhop-pimp father and the prostitute his father was managing at the time. The night of Jimmy's ninth birthday, however, another traumatic experience occurred. Jimmy's father was seriously disabled, and the prostitute was killed in a drunken-driving accident. With his father confined to the hospital for a long convalescence, Jimmy was placed in a local orphanage. His family life, such as it was, had come to an end. While one could speculate at length upon all of the possible consequences of this family life for Jimmy's subsequent career, one thing seems clear. His experience with this couple seems to have provided him with all of the necessary rationalizations for, and an understanding of, prostitution as an acceptable activity. It was to play an important part in his criminal activities. He had been effectively socialized.

For the next four years, Jimmy was in and out of a series of foster homes and welfare placements. At age thirteen, his official delinquency began, and he was confined in a training school. That began his apprenticeship in a long list of institutions, county, state, and federal. It is no wonder that he possesses some of the "convict's" ability and interest in "doing time."

His delinquent and criminal career from that time forward is too long to recite in detail. Briefly, he participated in the conflict gangs of the forties. He was involved, on one occasion, in a shooting incident. At age fourteen he was arrested on a reduced charge for violation of the Mann Act; he tried to place a sixteen-year-old girl in a house of prostitution in another state. At fifteen, he lied about his age to get into the merchant marines and was discharged after only three trips for defying authority. Still at the age of fifteen, he tried to manage a twenty-six-year-old prostitute whom he could not control, so he went back to the gang. During this phase, his period of incarceration, like his life in the gang, was characterized by aggressivity and constant trouble with authorities. When, however, he was sent to adult prison, he learned the value of "cool," stopped strong-arming, and turned to pimping, burglary, and heroin. By the age of twenty, he had made the "big-time," i.e., he was sent to a famous, maximum-security prison. Whatever skills he possessed as a professional criminal, however, seemed to have been counterbalanced by the problems related to his unprofessional addiction to heroin. For the next twelve years, he spent most of his time in jails and in state and federal prisons, usually, though not always, for activities related to the task of maintaining a habit.

When we encounter Dunn in this narrative, he is in his mid-twenties serving his second major incarceration as an adult. Several more were to follow.

CHARLES MURRAY

The life of Charles Murray, by contrast, is less unique, less spectacular. Even so, he scarcely fits a conventional mold. He is just the opposite of the middle-class ideal. He dresses and acts informally (in fact he often looks as though he slept in his clothes). He is generous to a fault, reflecting an antimaterialistic bias and a contempt for possessions. He is always present at work, but he is never organized—he hates organizational routine. The result is that he is almost as inept when it comes to paper work as he is when it comes to things mechanical—hopeless. And, while he is not an aggressive person, he is never reluctant to sound off or play the iconoclast when he feels the occasion demands.

He has two major interests aside from his work: books and food. He is an avid reader and a gourmet. In fact, it is with respect to the latter that the one chink in his personal philosophy is most evident. While, on one hand, he would be reluctant to attribute much virtue to any tradition, he is a snob when it comes to food and drink. So aristocratic are his tastes that he considers most people Philistines. And while, for example, he would never admit to having purchased domestic wines, he has been known to consume large quantities of such wine when furnished by others.

This behavior, much like Dunn's, seems to reflect Murray's background. Like Dunn, Murray had an unconventional childhood, the product of a charming, impractical, and completely irresponsible father who would start a small business and then expect everyone else to run it, a shrewd mother who kept the family intact, and a home in which, because of the Depression, there was not always enough to eat. These conditions seem to have increased his ability to identify with people in trouble.

Murray's subsequent life reflects his humanistic inclinations. He eventually entered an eastern university and specialized in Medieval history and philosophy. He financed his education by working for United Press International, yet always fostered the idea of working eventually with people in trouble, especially criminals.

After completing his education, he traveled extensively, working at a variety of jobs. For a two-year period, he was employed by a major international airline where his duties took him to many parts of Europe. Because he was trilingual (French-Italian-English), he enjoyed this work and had much to contribute to it.

His interest in criminals prevailed, however, and he eventually went to the West Coast to pursue studies in criminology. Following that, he entered correctional work, became interested in group techniques, and achieved considerable reputation because of his skills in that specialty, not only among correctional personnel, but among inmates, many of whom responded positively to him. Because of his unhappiness with prison conditions, however, he was constantly seeking change—a tendency which often put him at odds with his fellow workers and his superiors.

Frustrated because he was unable to do much about these problems in a large state system, he left that system and participated for a number of years in experimental correctional programs in the community. The events he describes herein occurred midway in his prison experiences. He is now studying and working in Europe, still in pursuit of elusive yet more effective ways of working with offenders.

Given Murray's unconventional background, he would seem to be better equipped to understand and work with people like Dunn than would most professionals. Yet, as one reads this book, he is struck by two things—the inability of the two men to communicate with each other on basic issues, and the extent to which the nature of prison life itself seems to dampen any chance that the problem can be resolved. Basic differences between the two men, plus the antithetical nature of their prison roles, seem to raise insurmountable barriers.

THE LACK OF COMMUNICATION

There are numerous examples of the inability of Dunn and Murray to communicate, but two are worth noting. The first is important because it raises the issue as to what Dunn's basic problems are and what should be done about them. Basically, Murray feels sorry for Dunn and sees him as a person who rejects other people and uses them, because he has experienced so much rejection himself. He has been badly hurt, says Murray, and reacts with an attitude of total distrust.

In addition, Murray feels that Dunn has serious sexual problems. "In all probability," he argues, "he [Dunn] would be a homosexual, except he cannot handle that kind of feeling. He is too busy telling the world how masculine he is, which explains why he spends so much time in keeping his body in trim while he's in prison" (p. 98).

Pursuing this line of reasoning, he observes Dunn and other prisoners working out in the gym with weights and concludes that it is little more than a homosexual game. Not only are they putting their muscles on display, but in the act of helping each other lift large weights, they are only just short of a sexual act. "I'll bet," says Murray, "that that guy on the bench has an erection" (p. 151). Carrying this interpretation even further, he expresses an opinion common among many correctional people, that heroin usage stems from sexual problems. Not only is the use of a needle and syringe symbolic of the sex act, but heroin serves as a substitute for women (p. 152).

Not only do some other correctional people, and certainly Dunn, see this interpretation as bizarre, but it raises questions regarding modes of intervention. Murray seems to imply that some sort of deep psychotherapy is in order, although he never makes this explicit.

By contrast, Dunn's attention to basic problems seems to be centered more directly on the nature of the prison itself, and the stupidity of correctional people and "Square Johns" in general. What these differences bring into focus is the historical division of criminological theory into alternative schools. Murray tends to emphasize the psychogenic school, with its concentration upon underlying pathology, while, alternatively, Dunn's behavior might be attributed to his early socialization and his lifelong experience in institutions. Role theory and differential identification with deviant patterns and associates would provide the explanation in this case.

The dilemma posed by alternative ways of seeing offenders is illustrated by the interaction between Murray and Dunn when Murray learns that Dunn's wife is divorcing him. Full of concern over the matter, Murray asks Dunn how he feels about the divorce, whether they had planned on having any children, all of the conventional questions. Despite his concern, however, Murray's solicitude could scarcely have been more off the mark. Dunn is upset all right, but not for any of the conventional or idealistic reasons one usually attributes to marriage. He is furious because his wife will no longer be sending him money while he is in prison, and he will have lost his means of support once he leaves. "She knows she's supposed to take care of me while I'm down," he thinks. "I'm sure I taught her that much. A good pimp doesn't care if a broad blows him while he's on the streets, it's part of the game. . . . But this broad was with me two years, and I made her my main old lady. She knows she's supposed to take care of me now that I can't take care of myself. Goddamn, stinkin' snake, wait 'til I get my hands on her!" (pp. 61-62).

Given the two frames of reference from which both men approached the issue, the two could scarcely have been communicating any less efficiently. But if understanding were to be enhanced, how could it be accomplished? Is Dunn's reaction best understood in terms of a basic, even pathological, rejection of all women, indeed all people, or is it more the result of his early socialization in an environment of pimping and prostitutes? Whichever interpretation one prefers, the problem was horrendous and was scarcely made better by the prison conditions in which they found themselves. So long as Murray had to deal with Dunn as a captive in total confinement, his efforts to alter Dunn's sense of rejection were mocked by daily and living proof of rejection. Since the conditions make the implementation of most theories of intervention difficult, let us consider them briefly.

THE PRISON SETTING

One of the first things the reader will encounter in subsequent discussions is that prison organization is fractured, not merely by staff-inmate differences, but by intra-staff conflicts as well. The official segment of the prison is not a unified system, but is torn by differing philosophies every bit as debilitating to correctional effectiveness as inmate resistances and subgroups. Official staff meetings are characterized not by unity and respect, but by scarcely concealed animosity and mutual disrespect. The difficulties among the staff are rooted not only in the conflict between punitive and treatment ideologies, but in the probable insolubility of the problems which they face. There is real question as to whether they can manage a large number of captives, in an environment of total security, in such a way as to achieve rehabilitative goals.

Not only does Murray find himself in perpetual conflict with Lieutenant Chuvalo, who symbolizes the custodial point of view, but with his fellow professionals whose interest in changing offenders seems to have been overwhelmed by the inherent difficulties of a large and impersonal system. The practical, day-to-day problems which they face seem to have overcome whatever idealistic inclinations they once may have possessed.

Their disillusionment seems to be due not just to the irascible obstructionism of a punitively-oriented administration, but to the questionable utility of treatment methods in a large, closed institution. As Cressey (1968: 33) has noted: "Correctional workers are called upon to play a game they cannot win." Their problems reflect an ambivalent society whose expectations are in conflict. While the public feels that the correctional system is inadequate, it is not eager to bring about change (compare with Joint Commission on Correctional Manpower and Training, 1968). Consequently, correctional organizations reflect this ambivalence, raising the question as to whether change can occur in a setting in which conflicting ideologies and staff groups are expected both to punish the offender and, at the same time, to rehabilitate him. Ironically, therefore, the likelihood is great that Chuvalo's cynicism is a more accurate reflection of the actual situation than is Murray's humanistic idealism.

Chuvalo is convinced that inmates, especially those like Dunn, are manipulators, and that strict controls, not treatment techniques, are the answer. One only plays into their hands by relaxing restrictions or allowing them to make decisions. Paradoxically, there is considerable confirmation for this in the pages which follow. It may be true that Chuvalo has a better understanding of what Dunn is doing, and why he is doing it, than does Murray. Murray prefers to believe that, given the chance, inmates like Dunn will exhibit concern for one another, will become involved in a rehabilitative process, and will help to reform the prison. Quite often, he recites the lamentable history of men like Dunn as a justification for the feeling that, if they are shown some of the respect and acceptance they have never received, they will respond positively. Unfortunately, given the character of the present system, Dunn reveals few such inclinations. While he hates Chuvalo, he has little but contempt for Murray. The latter, to him, is simply soft-headed, a person who, because of his idealism, is a much easier "mark" than Chuvalo. He has the same feeling, incidentally, for other treatment personnel, holding them if anything in even greater contempt.

In one revealing, even shocking incident, Murray describes a group therapy session in which a frustrated inmate blurts out his perception of the treatment director, Mr. Small. Reflecting his clinical training, Small always attempts to remain kindly, yet cool and detached in his dealings with inmates, to respond with soft answers and analytical skills to their extreme provocations. In reacting to this soft demeanor, the inmate tells Small that he reminds him of a "broad," that he would like nothing better than to fuck him. The gleeful response of the other inmates to his statement reveals that this is not an isolated opinion, or at least that they are full of frustration and anger generated by the obviously inappropriate character of highly profes- sionalized behaviors in a harsh and degrading environment. Rather than resolving problems, those behaviors only add to them. They are totally incongruent with reality. Thus the suffocating character of such an environment chokes everyone. Coupled with all of the other custodial and management problems which they face, officials, like in- mates, are trapped in a setting conducive more to animosity and manipulation than to collaboration and change.

There is, of course, an inmate system in any prison which is a counterpart to the official system which has just been described. Much has been made in the correctional literature of the need to bridge the gap between these two systems so that the adoption of prosocial points of view by inmates can be facilitated, but Dunn's discussion makes it clear why such a bridging is extremely difficult. Dunn indicates that one of the worst things an inmate can do is to be seen talking to the "bulls"—the guards. He notes the futile attempts of Murray and other treatment staff to get inmates in group sessions to discuss the stabbing of one inmate by another, or a fight between a Black and a White, by appealing to their humanitarian impulses and the need for a safe and humane environment. Murray also is angry because staff members will not submit themselves, in group meetings, to the same confrontation regarding their motives and behaviors to which they expect inmates to submit. Dunn is aware that inmates prey upon each other, and that there is continual danger not only from possible inmate power struggles but from deranged individuals as well. Yet he is uncompromising in his adherence to the inmate code. Fur- thermore, this is not an isolated adherence; it is shared by other inmates far more legitimately-oriented than he. Why should this be? Why should other inmates, often with much more to lose than has a habitual offender like Dunn, be so unyielding?

The answer, of course, lies in the fact that the prison system is a caste system. The rules which govern staff-inmate relations favor separation and accommodation, not collaboration and assimilation. The roles of captive and captor are mutually exclusive. The result, therefore, is that even prosocial inmates may have more to lose than to gain by open cooperation with the official caste.

This problem is frightfully complex, possessed of a host of ramifications. The most obvious is the fact that an inmate who associates openly with "bulls," or is candid in group meetings, may not only suffer a lack of prestige and acceptance among other inmates, but may see his personal safety jeopardized as well. He is an open threat to the whole system of norms which govern inmate relations, and to those who occupy positions of power within the inmate system. But the ramifications do not end there. Paradoxically, efforts to bridge the boundaries between inmate and official castes can be a serious threat to officials as well. Many of the deviant or inhumane practices which occur in prisons cannot occur without the tacit acceptance of officials. In the interest of maintaining order, officials must share some power with inmates, and in so doing permit inmate leaders to exercise their own brand of controls over other inmates. Furthermore, there is the very real possibility that if relations were opened up, and this system of controls jeopardized, there would be serious disruptions, at least at the outset. And when disruptions occur, usually in the form of riot, prison officials are subject to the unthinking reactions of politicians and ordinary citizens who are far more interested in control than in rehabilitation. That is why officials, like inmates, are supportive of the notion that an inmate should "do his own time" and refrain from involvement in matters that "don't concern him." That is why, furthermore, staff members, like Murray, who constantly strive to change the nature of the caste system, encounter resistance from their peers as well as from inmates. Any person, inmate or staff, who threatens the subtle balance of power that exists in a prison is resisted.

To be sure, there are ways available for the inmate who wishes to reveal information to do so. But those ways are covered by the rules of the game as well. Not only must he remain anonymous, but the rewards he receives for his information must likewise remain covert. Everyone despises the informer, including officials, but they must take steps to protect him.

Given this state of affairs, then, Dunn's emphasis upon keeping to himself, remaining cool, and appearing to conform to official rules, makes a lot of sense. Even the legitimately-oriented inmate has more to lose than to gain by attempting to deal openly with the things he sees going on around him. After all, suppose he were to try to change things. What would there be in it for him? So long as he is an inmate, there is no way of changing that status within the system. Could he ever aspire to become a teacher in the prison, a counselor, or a work supervisor and to have that change sanctioned by the system in the form of an official title and such customary prequisites of a job as a salary, insurance, and a retirement plan? The fact is that there is no upward mobility, no climbing from inmate to official caste. If he is to do these desirable things, he must wait until he leaves the system. In fact, the prohibition against doing them within the system extends even to the parole status of an offender when he leaves the prison. In the state in which Dunn was a prisoner, official rules prohibit any fraternization between offenders and correctional personnel. Such rules, of course, supposedly help to protect officials from corruption by offenders, but they also serve to maintain the caste system, leaving unanswered the question as to how inmates can acquire nondeviant associates and learn prosocial points of view in the absence of institutionalized means and support. Thus, any inmate is forced to accept his inmate status, even if he does not believe in it. Unless he conforms to the rules of the caste system, he may be in serious trouble—even worse than he is in already.

This is a bleak picture of the prison. Indeed, critics like Goffman (1961) are highly pessimistic about the chances of converting places of confinement into effective correctional organizations. Prisons are striking examples of the problems posed by conflicting punitive and reform ideologies. They are so full of logical contradictions that, while they effectively suppress the offender, they can do little to change him. Yet it is also a fact that society does not have proven alternatives, especially where the serious offender is concerned. Thus one is given pause by the necessity for concern about protection of the community as well as rehabilitation of the offender. But rather than speculating further on this dilemma here, let us turn to the experiences of Dunn and Murray. They will shed further light on the question. Then, when their narration is completed, we can return to it and reflect upon it in terms of existing scientific findings.

Chapter 1

Life
in Prison

DUNN:

The New Game Begins

The first thing is the light. Consciousness comes fast in the penitentiary. The bull throws the master switch in the cell-block and each cell is flooded with light. I know the bull is a sadist. He enjoys his work. He wakes us up every morning at six o'clock with the jar of a hundred watts, while it's still dark outside, knowing we have no place to go. It's probably all part of the program, or their so-called treatment. They say they don't punish people in prisons anymore, they rehabilitate them. But they have a long way to go to convince me.

So each morning I pull the coarse sheets and state blanket a littler higher over my head trying to escape the light and curse the bull. The first thing I think is, "That son-of-a-bitch." The saddest thing is I can't tell him what I think. Of course, some guys regularly call the bulls a sack of whatever it is they think they are. But that's not really the smart way. All they do is throw you in the hole, and as if that's not bad enough, it adds time to your stay. But I do get something out of knowing that he's less than I am. A prison guard is the lowest thing in the world and has been for all time.

Waking up in a cell is an old story now. It was a different penitentiary last time, but cells always look the same. They rarely send you back to the same place in this system. And they've got so many in this state that it's no problem. Besides, they have a built-in graduating system. A guy normally starts in the "country club" in the southern part of the state. Next time he goes a little farther north for medium security. From there it's on to the "Big Top," what they call their close security prison. And the final stop on the list is really the end of the road, the "Fortress," and just the name alone is enough to make most guys want to stay out of it.

But they all look pretty much the same. Most of them have the same furniture; the supplies all come out of the same pot. The bed is a steel frame bolted to the wall. The springs are heavy wire that give little comfort. The mattress label says it's stuffed with cotton fiber, but it feels like straw. Where the state gets them is anybody's guess, but they'd better not lose their connection, because it can't be accidental and must also be part of the treatment. The sheets feel like burlap and are manufactured in one of the other joints in the system. I was in that one last time. The clothing manufacturing is part of what they call their "vocational training" program. But what they teach you is how to get along in the penitentiary. They teach you a lifetime penitentiary trade so you'll always be useful to them when you come back the next time, and the next time. They won't ever have to retrain you. They only manufacture maintenance materials and supplies for themselves and the other state institutions. On paper it looks good. They are able to say they're teaching trades to convicts: trades like the textile mill, clothing manufacturing, and furniture manufacturing. A textile mill trade would be fine if we were in the South, or at least in the East, because that's where most of them are. But we're in an "enlightened state," where they don't have textile mills, and most other kinds of slave labor, so they're actually teaching us a nonexistent trade. And clothing manufacturing, that's a real laugh! What they do is teach you how to make prison clothes, and you can get quite good at making them. The only problem is after you've learned the trade here you can't get a job doing it outside. State specifications, by which they manufacture things, aren't exactly competitive in the open market! And what you've been taught isn't good enough for the higher standards on the outside. All you can learn is to make prison clothes—so the only place you can get a job at the trade they teach you is in the penitentiary. And the same thing goes for their other trades. Of course, they have displays of "prison-made" articles in prominent places for the public outside of the prisons, but they're just cream, individual efforts, and the system neither wants nor encourages excellence.

The rest of the cell isn't much better. It's ten feet long, four and a half feet wide, and eight feet high, solid cement.

There's a locker beside the bed in which to keep my "personals." *Personals*, that's another joke—how personal can anything be when the bull has the only key and is in there regularly shaking it down? Anything really personal isn't where they can find it.

A combination toilet with a small sink over it, bolted to the wall, just inside the door, completes the physical layout of the cell. It's sparkling clean; I keep it that way. I'd better, because the bull makes sure it's clean. It seems that prison administrators are very concerned with how clean the toilets are.

The walls are a pastel rose. I understand many years ago somebody who was supposed to be an expert told the administration that pastel colors help to soothe savage convicts! By now the rose is beginning to look more and more bilious. I think I'd be better satisfied with the traditional gray. If you're a convict, you're a convict, and calling a convict an inmate, or painting walls rose instead of gray, doesn't change anything.

In fact, another funny thing, the department won't let us be called convicts anymore. They feel it's too undignified a term. By order of the director, we're all inmates now, not convicts. But he doesn't know that we still think of ourselves as convicts and for somebody to call another guy in the penitentiary an inmate is the same thing as calling him a snitch.

I'm glad I'm a convict. I wouldn't have it any other way. This is the way I want it. They can call me what they want, but I know what I am. Sometimes it's confusing. I don't particularly like the day-to-day world of the penitentiary, but at the same time it's my world, the one I know best, and in a way I enjoy it.

I often wonder if Joe Square out on the streets, with a fat, nagging wife and four runny-nosed kids, a dirty job where he gets greasy all day, ever hates his job. Can he actually believe it's the only way for him?

In many ways I'm better off than Joe Square. This is the age of enlightened penology. They don't whip your ass anymore; they feed you three times a day; and they give you a crummy cell. Still, I don't have to worry about taxes, bills, and whether my neighbor thinks I'm a good guy or not.

I know what I am. I'm a convict and nothing the state can do can make me change, because I know I got the better go. I've got something that most guys, especially the Joe Squares, don't have. I've got hope! I've got the streets, and I'm going out there again. I've got something to look forward to. Joe Square has the rut, the routine, and there's no hope for him. When I get out there again I can make up for everything that's happening to me now. I'll be free, free to live the way I want and to do what I want. I know Joe Square can't make that statement. I can shoot dope, steal, rob, pimp whores. I can live as fast and as good as I want. And when they nail me again, I can come back "home" for a vacation and wait it out until the next time. But I'll always have the knowledge that I'll get out again, and again, and again. So I can do the time they give me, this time and the next time. The judge who gave me this jolt thought he was hurting me, but he doesn't know that I'll live to piss on his grave!

So I'll get up this morning, like every other morning, and I'll go through the routine, because the routine is what saves me. The days are all the same. Each one exactly like the one preceding it and like the one following it. They're all the same—just a blur—and looking back a year ago when I got this jolt, it seems like only yesterday because yesterday was just like it was a year ago.

* * *

I finally get up and put on my *bonaroo* clothes, special starched jobs that cost me four packs a week. To most people they probably look like nothing more than blue denims, neat as denims can be. But here they mean you're "clean." If you're sharp on the outside, you've gotta be sharp on the inside, too, and just because everyone has to wear the same clothes, you can still set yourself off as different by being a good enough hustler to be able to afford having your clothes specially done. The con with the concession in the laundry separates my clothes when they come in, does them special, and sends them back through normal channels.

Then I wash and comb my hair. Next I' look around the cell, make sure I've got everything that I'll need for the day, because I can't get back into my cell until the noon count. Next I stand by the door; after double checking to make sure no contraband is lying around, I wait for the bull to throw the bar running along the top of the cell doors so my door will open.

When the bull throws the bar I step out of the cell and start looking down on the cellblock floor for my partner, Tommy. I'm on the third tier and Tommy's on the first, so he always gets out before I do. The cellblock is noisy, I suppose because the convicts are free from their cells. The convicts who were let out with me push past, hurrying to get the state dole, the breakfast provided by the great mother, the state.

They put more guys in the penitentiary in this state than they do in lots of others combined. And it's hard for them to let you loose once they get their hands on you. They make sure you have plenty of parole when you leave so you can violate one of their petty parole rules, and they can get you back quickly, without having to give you the benefit of a court trial. But they can also make their boast that they treat their convicts better than any other state! They do everything for you: they protect you, coddle you, and are very angry and surprised when you don't do just as they want. When there's a riot in one of their joints, they're dumbfounded and don't know what to do. They react as a parent would to a hard-headed and little-understood child. At first they become punitive to handle their anger, but then they feel guilty, and soon they have everything back as it was before. And when they're putting things back, they do it with the attitude, "Now you boys won't be bad and do that again, will you?" Maybe someday they'll wake up and realize that they are dealing with destroyers: men whose only purpose is to destroy things and who are only functional and operative when they are destroying something, or someone.

I want nothing from the state that they want to give me. All I want is the opportunity to hate them and to destroy everything they stand for and everyone who gets in my way.

I'm going to do everything I can, all my life, to beat them, rob them, lie, and con them. I'm going to beat them at their own game. I'll play it like they want it while they've got their eyes on me; but as soon as they turn their backs, or can't see me, I'll kill something that someone thinks is good.

Junk is the hottest thing they're after now. I wonder if it strikes them as significant that a great percentage of the guys in the prisons in this state are either there for junk or for other crimes to get money to buy junk? That's what they want least, but that's what they're getting. We're all going to beat them at their own game!

Speaking of junk, Tommy told me yesterday that some junk is supposed to hit the institution today, but I don't know. It seems like everyday Tommy's got some hot wire that junk's supposed to hit. I think that's what keeps him going. He's constantly hustling for smack. Each day is another in a long series of eternal quests for junk. His whole life in the penitentiary—and outside, when he's there —revolves around when he can get high and what he can get high on.

Tommy's a good guy, got a good name—he's never snitched on anyone. And I suppose he's my best friend here. But all the same I don't trust him. He's so kinky it's pitiful. Anybody who's that hung-up on junk just can't be trusted. He looks just like the stereotype of the dope fiend: five feet ten inches tall, skinny, with bad posture and stoop-shoulders. He's not a bad-looking guy otherwise, in a dark, quiet, intense way. But at the same time he exudes the message that he can't be trusted. He's the kind of a guy that you're always watching when he's in your house, to see what he's doing.

By this time I know his whole story—what he is like, who he is, and what he's liable to do. He comes from a so-called "good" family. His father's a respected business-man, and a Lieutenant-Colonel in the Army Reserves. His mother died when he was young and his father has since remarried twice. They always lived in nice, respectable, upper-middle-class homes. They started the kid on piano lessons when he was six years old, and by the time he was in high school, he was playing at small, local jazz clubs. I don't know who put the first needle in his arm, but it must have been what he was looking for, because he hasn't looked back since.

I don't know, I must be a different kind of a junky than he is. Junk doesn't make up my whole life. I'll believe there's junk here when I see it. When the man comes to me and says, "I got it good, baby," I ask him what's the price, and if I got the bread I buy it. If I don't have the money, I don't get the junk. It's not that big of a thing in the penitentiary to me, anyway. Outside I'm steadily running for stuff. But I think the reason for that is that it gives me something to do. Here I've already got something to do. I've got to do this time for the state; then I can get out and do what I want.

While I walk down the enclosed stairs with the guys from my tier, I don't say anything to them and they don't say anything to me. That's the way it's always been: "You do your own time." But at the same time I notice a difference since the last jolt. At the "Top" it was doubtful if I knew thirty guys in the entire population of five thousand. But here they've got that goddamn group therapy business going and I know everybody's name, at least in my cellblock. The groups are changing the prisons. I don't want to know these hoosiers' names. They're nothing more than broken-down, left-footed thieves who couldn't get their hands in a rain barrel! They think they're thieves because they're in the penitentiary. Most of them shouldn't even be here. In group you find out about them. They're always crying about their messed-up wives or mothers, and most of them are here for throwing a brick through a jewelry store window just to get away. They're not really thieves, or pimps, or dope fiends, and I want nothing to do with them.

By the time I get down on the cellblock floor, most of the guys have already left—which is good because I like to miss the crowd. Tommy is standing by the door waiting for me. Fields, the cellblock bull, is standing over at his station, near the little desk in the front of the cellblock where the phone and emergency controls are. I've been here a year and all that time Fields has been the day-watch officer. We've yet to exchange a word, other than the necessary ones that his "duty" calls upon him to address to me. I look at him when I go by with the dead expression I use for bulls, and I often wonder if he's even vaguely aware of how much I hate him, the son-of-a-bitch. He doesn't have to say anything for me to hate him. All he has to do is to be who he is and wear that green uniform. That's enough.

In fact the easiest way to get a bad name in the penitentiary is to talk to bulls. That's one of the rules: you don't talk to bulls, and bulls include anyone in the penitentiary who doesn't have a number. The best way to get along in the joint is to completely ignore the staff. Act as though they're not there. It's really pretty easy, too. Everything that a convict wants is only available from other convicts. The bulls can't do anything for you. Moreover, it's best to stay out of their faces—the less they know about you, the better off you are. They already know too much about you anyway from the police reports. So the best way is not to make it any worse. If you stay away from them and don't even let them know you're in the joint, one day they'll wake up and say to themselves, "Say, is that Dunn still here? He's been here long enough and I haven't heard anything of him, so he must have really straightened up. I guess we'd better let him go." So there's a good reason for every convict rule in the penitentiary. It's taken centuries for them to evolve, and each one is based on the personal experiences of thousands of convicts, and they're passed on so that each succeeding generation of convicts will be able to do his time that much easier.

Tommy starts with his junk-talk as soon as we get outside of the unit and start up the hall. He just knows he's going to score today.

"This is it, man, I know it," he says. "I talked to Lalo just before lock-up last night, and he told me, 'This is the day.'"

"Has Lalo ever given you a right steer yet?" I want to prick his balloon a little. Lalo's another one of those junk-sick nuts whose whole life is heroin.

"Yeah, yeah, I know about Lalo. He's a bum-steer, all right, but he's never burned anybody. And I'm not taking any chances. I don't know about you, but if any junk ever gets here I want to be in on it."

There is nothing to answer to that. Gut-convictions can't be shaken, and he's going to believe what he wants to. If he wants to believe that he's going to get loaded today, then that's what he going to believe.

The hallway, from which the various cellblocks and units branch off, is a quarter of a mile long. The messhall is located just about in the middle, across from the Control and Custody Offices. Bulls are standing about every thirty feet along the corridor, watching the guys and harrassing them, telling them to walk two abreast if they bunch up. It's a dismal, foreboding-looking corridor, with its undulating mass of blue denim bodies, interspersed with the vague green of the bulls. The bulls think they're running the penitentiary, but they don't have the vaguest notion of what's going on here.

When we walk by the Control Office, I see Murray, the unit counselor, standing there. I can't help thinking to myself, "Good God, it's seven in the morning, what's that fool doing here already?" I guess he doesn't have anything better to do. I hear a lot of these so-called "inmates" saying that he's supposed to be a hell of a guy. But to me he's just an idiot. Why anyone would volunteer to spend a third of his life in a penitentiary is beyond me.

We turn in at the messhall, are greeted by the usual din, and stand in the line leading to the steam tables.

The pressure of this penitentiary is immense. And it's particularly noticeable in the mess hall. The mess hall is clean and functional-looking with its tile floor and half-tile

walls. There's also a big, inspiring mural painted by one of
the convicts. I'm sure it's another instance of that psycho-
logically oriented fool the state hired at one time or
another to provide some aesthetic beauty in the penitentiary.

The line leading to the serving tables stretches down the
middle of the dining hall, and there are four-man tables on
both sides. There's room for eight hundred men in the mess
hall at one time; and that's all they want there at any one
time—more would be dangerous in case of a riot. So they
have to stagger the units to eat, and it takes about an hour
and a half to feed the whole joint.

The mess hall is as noisy as usual, with the clanging of
metal utensils on the aluminum trays. Standing in that line
you really feel as though you're on display. Convicts from
both sides are sitting there eating and looking at you to see
what you're going to do. If trouble happens, it's usually in
the mess hall and those damn trays make good weapons:
they can split your head open with one. And the pressure
is so immense that all it really takes is for one nut to blow
his stack and go after a guy in the mess hall, and then
there's no telling what can happen. And the joint is full of
nuts. You don't know if one of the hoosiers you're next to
is a psychopathic killer.

I hate to come to the damn mess hall, but it's the only
store in town, and if I want to eat, I have to do it here.

After we get our food and come down the other side of
the aisle by the wall and find an empty place to sit,
Tommy goes on with his story. He's sure the shit's going to
hit here today. He tells me that Blake, the free man, the
second cook in the kitchen, is supposed to make his run
today and bring in some stuff. I've often wondered why
the idiots who make runs, "mules" we call them, take such
chances. Blake gets fifty to one hundred dollars when he

makes a run, depending on how much stuff he brings. He makes one or two runs a month, so he picks up a hundred or two hundred extra bucks a month. If they bust him with a pocket full of heroin, he's going to be here with all the rest of us thinking about how he shouldn't have done it. But I guess old Barnum was right: a sucker's born every minute.

But, as I listen to Tommy go on with his story, I know nothing's going to happen today. He's going to run around all day, convinced the junk's here, and by tonight he'll have another "hot wire" that the junk'll be here tomorrow. In the meantime, I'll go to work in that goddamned welding shop, as I do every day, and go through the routine, eat dinner, and get locked up at 4:30. Then I'll get up to-morrow and begin the whole process all over again.

Life
at Prison

MURRAY:

I live on the prison grounds. My sparsely furnished, single room with little privacy and no bath is called "staff quarters." Actually the rooms are little better than the cells in the self-contained buildings which house the 3,700 inmates. A man can serve many years and never have to step outside to see the light of day.

I first got into this business five years ago. I suppose the reason had something to do with wanting to help the underdog; or maybe I had seen too many Humphrey Bogart

movies. Perhaps I even felt sorry for the inmates. At any
rate, I joined the system, that great all-embracing, protective mother of them all, Civil Service: a mother from whom
all civil servants draw continuous nourishment, reassurance,
and above all, security. In effect, it has become a modern-
day form of love.

I first went to work in the department at the intensive
care facility: it is staffed with a high ratio of professional
persons utilizing the latest medical, chemical, and psychological treatment techniques. For a new person in the
correctional business, it was a fascinating experience.
Shortly after that I was transferred here because of my
"expertness" in the group method and also to further my
professional development. I was to implement the group
technique at this prison.

                    *   *   *

This morning, as I approach the gate, the man in the
guntower asks me to identify myself. His voice blares at me
from the high outside speaker. I answer. Either he's a new
man or he doesn't recognize me. But he's probably unusually nervous this morning anyway because of the heavy
fog. The prisoners are kept locked up in their cellblocks
until the fog lifts. There have been a number of escapes
during foggy weather, so prison officials and guards remain
rather tense until the fog lifts. Then the final "fog count"
is taken once again, and the "count-is-clear" whistle is
sounded.

Then it will begin again: a struggle, battle, rehabilitation,
game, tragedy, punishment—call it what you will. I guess
it's really two different things: the way the staff sees it,
and the way the inmates see it. The staff thinks that,
through a magical process, some kind of change in the

individual man will take place. This includes group-counseling sessions, coupled with vocational training ("Everyone must have a trade.") and educational courses ("It's important to have a high school diploma in order to get a job."). But, of course, at the same time, the more important thing is that the inmates are kept busy and trouble is kept at a minimum. The inmates think of prison, and use it, as a second home—a safe place where they can talk about their criminal activity, recoup their health, and talk about the unfair way life has treated them. Further, it is a place where they can get away from wife or mother, and all other responsibilities.

The inmate uses the prison system. He actually gets the staff to believe that he will change his ways, that he will learn a trade, that he will "go out there and do right." He says he is tired of these places and he doesn't want to keep coming back. In many cases he will learn a trade in prison that is technologically outmoded, such as welding or shoe repair, and discover he can't support himself. Or else, if he's educationally qualified, he will go into something complicated, like electronics or aero-mechanics, discovering after he is released that he doesn't care for it, or doesn't want to start at $2.00 per hour when everyone else is making $5.00, or that he can't get security clearance to work in a defense plant where these skills are in demand.

Then there is the inmate who tells you "why" he violated probation, or "why" he failed parole and came back on a new beef. Most of the "whys" have to do with the pressures of the outside: he couldn't get a decent job; nobody wanted to hire an ex-con; his wife was a nagging bitch; he ran out of money and just had to do something, so he robbed the corner liquor store, or pushed a little "stuff" in order to get some money to keep himself going.

Nobody can touch the inmate. He is safe from everyone

except other inmates. The Internal Revenue Service and the inmates are strangers. Creditors find it difficult, if not impossible, to collect from him. Public welfare agencies are caring for his wife and children often far better than he ever did himself.

The officers coming off the first watch, as I near them, look pretty tired. Night work is not easy, especially on the late shift. The inmates are asleep when they come on, and are barely getting up when they go off. They must feel useless, for all they can do is play baby-sitter to a group of sleeping men. Their job consists of taking two or three counts, flashing lights through the bars on the sleeping faces to make sure they haven't lost anyone.

There is, of course, a minimal contact with some inmates, mostly cooks and kitchen workers who get up early to prepare breakfast, who are neither communicative nor receptive. Some officers like it that way and prefer not to be involved with the inmates. Others prefer the shift because they are attending college during the day in an attempt to better their status and job at the prison. Still others are on that shift for disciplinary reasons, usually for having offended a sergeant, lieutenant, or captain. How is that for a hierarchy of titles? They even have a watch commander in charge of the second and third watches.

Also following the military procedures, the regular line officers do not have any distinguishing features on their uniforms. They consist of dark green pants, matching Eisenhower jackets, and military-type caps, with khaki shirts and green ties. Many officers wear a break-away tie so that they cannot be garrotted with it by the inmates, whom they don't trust.

The senior officers are distinguishable from their underlings by a display of insignia. They wear the same type of uniform, except in place of the leather band over the visor on the cap, they have silver and gold bands. In addition, the sergeants wear small silver insignia with three green chevrons on their collars. The lieutenants wear a silver bar on their collars and the captain, a gold one.

The associate wardens and the warden wear suits. This enables them to present a businesslike image to the public. The present warden, Mr. Edward Cokely, is a reformed alcoholic who wears his suit like a farmer, which was his previous occupation.

Although Cokely supposedly means well, he has more trouble with his staff than any other warden in the system. For instance, he has a fetish about coffee breaks. You might think that as an ex-alcoholic he would encourage a lot of coffee drinking, as they do at Alcoholics Anonymous meetings, where they are always shoving coffee and dough-nuts at you. Not old man Cokely. He allows two breaks, one at 10:00 A.M. and the other at 2:30 P.M.

After passing through the big double doors of the ad-ministration building, I immediately run into Cokely in the hallway. He is a tall, well-built man with a countrified look, a craggy face with a red, bulbous nose, splotchy com-plexion, and small, penetrating eyes. His shock of white hair gives him a fatherly look which he has capitalized on to its fullest extent. He still has the dry martini voice, though he does his best to tone it down.

"Good morning, Mr. Cokely."

"Morning, Murray. Ready to do a good day's work after a restful weekend?" I wonder what he thinks we do with our weekends? I bet he supposes we all attend church and spend Sundays with our families, like he does.

"I'm ready to grind out a few Board reports. There isn't much else I can do with a case load of five hundred."

"There never seems to be enough staff," he says, "and someday I hope we get those extra positions. In the meantime, we have to depend on hard workers like you to get those Board reports out on time. Can't keep the Parole Board waiting, you know."

"What a lot of crap," I think, continuing on through the hallway toward the main corridor of the prison. Mustn't keep those political appointees waiting! Got to complete the ritual of writing thirty to forty Board reports summarizing the "progress" for each inmate scheduled to appear before the Parole Board. Each report reads much like the previous one, with very little having changed. An inmate may have a few more high school credits since his appearance last year, or be enrolled in a trade program (the fact that he already may have two or three "trades" has little bearing), but little else.

As a matter of fact I don't think Cokely or for that matter many of the staff is particularly interested in programs which change inmates so that they can stay out of prison. Cokely seems to respond to what society says it wants its prisons to be: places of punishment where men "learn their lesson." His major interest is in running a trouble-free, smooth institution, one that doesn't get into the newspapers because of riots. I think this is why they brought me and a few others here and started having daily therapy group meetings. The prison can then call itself a "therapeutic community." The method as it is used in prison, though, is mostly to control the inmates. I suppose it's "therapeutic" in a sense, only I don't know who's getting the most benefit, the inmates or the administration! The staff discovered it could run a smoother institution, and in the process convinced itself that there was some benefit for the inmate.

Entering the main corridor by the Control Office, where all prison activity is coordinated, I notice the men are just returning from breakfast. As they file out of the mess halls across from the Control Office, they light their morning cigarettes. There is a no smoking rule in the mess halls which prevents any dawdling over coffee. "Eat and go" is the rule. In some institutions within the system, each man in the row must finish eating before that row is given a hand signal to leave. But this is one of the modern prisons. When a man is finished eating, he leaves on his own. This particular mess hall—indeed this entire prison—is fairly new. The administrators and architects tried to humanize the dining area by using four-seat tables rather than the traditional long tables. The seats are still cemented to the floor, which prevents their being used as weapons. Of course, in the event of a riot, the men can still use the aluminum trays.

The mess hall, with its high ceiling, has pale yellow walls and a red tile floor. The place is usually clean and odorless. There is a massive mural on one wall depicting an early frontier scene. It was painted by a particularly eccentric but talented inmate, Joe Ying, the only Chinese inmate in the entire prison. I say "eccentric" because he stayed pretty much to himself. He didn't seem to like his fellow prisoners. I guess they didn't like him much, either. He worked himself into the honor wing, which meant that he could have a single cell. He worked in the hospital and became the chief surgical assistant to old Dr. Mallory, which meant that Ying could practically write his own ticket as far as his schedule was concerned. He didn't even have to attend the daily groups. He didn't believe in expressing his private feelings. In fact, he always insisted that he had done nothing wrong. And perhaps in terms of his culture he hadn't. When anyone asked about his crime, he would simply say that he was imprisoned for being a businessman. He was apparently well educated, and if you persisted in asking about his crime, he would eventually tell

you that he was merely following the law of supply and
demand. Consequently, he was a businessman! Then he
would give you his slow, quiet smile and walk off—quite a
character.

While standing in front of the mess hall thinking of Joe
Ying, I remember we are having Classification Committee
today. This is always a hard day for everyone, staff and
inmates alike. At best, the Classification Committee makes
educated guesses about what to do with an inmate while he
is in prison. At worst, it is another ritual to go through.

Lieutenant Chuvalo will be on the committee today. I
make a mental note not to antagonize him again before the
committee meeting. Otherwise, he'll take it out on my
cases. He really exploits that uniform and title he's so
proud of. Rumor has it that he has his uniform tailor-made;
anyway, he keeps it immaculate. His appearance is the very
paragon of the upright military man, complete with the
brilliant, glass shine of his shoes (which he acquires every
day from the inmate shoeshine stand—another state employee fringe benefit, along with the staff housing, barber
shop, dry cleaning, and car wash, all at minimal cost).

As soon as I turn into the Custody Corridor, which
houses all of the custody offices, I can tell it is going to be
one of those days, for the first person I meet is Chuvalo.

"Morning, Lieutenant," I say. "How are things?"

"O.K., I guess," he answers, "considering we're working
with a lot of convicts who think the world owes them a
living.

"Murray," he goes on, "I understand you're thinking of
starting a new small therapy group for sex offenders."

"That's right, Lieutenant. I had a similar group at the
intensive treatment unit, and I had a lot of success with it.
I thought I would make it voluntary, and in that way
attract only the men who are motivated to do something

about their problems. What do you think of the idea?"

"Not much," he says. "You know how these new-fangled ideas go. Programs, groups, special classes, special trades, here today and gone tomorrow. This is a bad business we're in and every day the inmate gets smarter and smarter. We do more and more for him and get less and less in return. Custody seems to be losing its grip, not only with the inmates, but with the treatment staff."

For a minute I am almost afraid he's going to get nostalgic about the good old days, when custody had complete control over the lives and destinies of the men and the prisons. But I should know him better.

"I suppose you guys think you have all the answers, huh? But let me tell you, I've been in this business twenty years and I don't see any changes. The statistics remain the same: fifty percent failure! You guys keep setting up your precious programs, and the men keep failing. And we keep building bigger and bigger institutions."

"Careful, Lieutenant," I laugh, "you're beginning to sound cynical like me!"

"No," he protests, taking me seriously, "I'll never be as way-out as you. You're a real nut. Coming in on your own time, working extra for these guys. They don't appreciate it." He puts his hand on my arm. "And someday they're going to take advantage of you."

"Well, thanks for the advice, Lieutenant." I can only conclude that he believes everything he says. "I'd better be getting upstairs so I can get some work done. I'll see you at classification."

While walking away from him, I begin thinking of what I have to do today. The first thing is an interview with Jimmy Dunn. Now there's a challenge! Young, intelligent, good-looking, with all the makings of an athlete, a businessman, or even an actor. But so far he's parlayed a youth offender sentence into the adult class, partly because he's so stubborn and rigid that he always wants his own way, and partly because he's so entrenched in the prison system that it has practically become a way of life. The only people he knows are other delinquents, both in and out of prison. I don't see how we can hope to compete with that kind of an orientation unless we completely revamp the system.

Suddenly I feel a slap on my back. At first I think it is one of the younger inmates, who are always testing staff. But it is only Bob Harris, like some inmates, a product of the system.

Bob has been a counselor, Grade I, for fifteen years, and at this point has resigned himself to never getting a promotion. He is fifty pounds overweight. "State Ass" the inmates call him. He always carries cookies that his wife bakes the day before. He has a penchant for them and thinks everyone else should too. Frankly, I detest them. If I refuse them, he looks at me as if I'm un-American or something. His coat pocket is generally bulging with Oh Henry candy bars, which he also dearly loves.

What do you do with a guy like Harris? The system protects him. Under the state Civil Service regulations you can't even fire him for being incompetent. It's almost impossible to be fired from the system, unless, of course, you're indiscreet enough to get caught bringing in booze, weed, or narcotics to an inmate. The only other cause for immediate dismissal is to be caught red-handed with the wife of an inmate. It's not like the federal system, where probation and parole officers can be dropped for incompetence. Their initial selection procedures are also much more stringent. But I suppose Bob can't help it. They say he grinds out a Board report in five minutes. I can well believe it after fifteen years of practice. Perhaps there's even something to be said for Bob's approach: give up the idea of promotion, collect your eight hundred dollars each month, plus all the fringe benefits, and don't get ulcers! At least he doesn't live on the prison grounds; he hasn't beat that to death. He lives in the nearby thriving metropolis of twenty-nine thousand, which at that, I guess, is better than living in either of the other two one-horse towns in this valley. One of them has two banks (a tribute to the thrift of the farmers), but unpaved streets!

I am thankful that Bob doesn't stop and talk to me, but continues on into the Classification Office.

When I arrive at the gate leading up to my office, I see that my old friend, John Galsworth, who seems to be a fixture at this gate lately (he must have offended someone), is on duty.

"Hi, John. How are things?" John's a guy who's easy to like. "Let me in my magic room so I can dispense some hocus-pocus and cure a few people."

"You are an optimist, Charlie." He gives me that big grin he's famous for, with the prominent, shining gold cap. "After what happened to me yesterday, I don't wonder that the inmates are suspicious of us."

"Come on up to the office and tell me about it."

"See what I mean? You *are* an optimist! I don't have the freedom of movement around here that you have. I have to stand at this gate all day and make sure none of the inmates get by to you counselors upstairs without authorization. In fact, I'm as much of a prisoner around this damn place as the men are!"

"Well, what's the trouble, John?"

"Have you really got a minute, Charlie? Let me tell you right here."

He launches into his story with a vengeance. As he talks about it, he seems to get more and more excited. "I've

been working the visiting room extra for the past two
weeks, just for the half hour that the visitors leave. Sergeant Bothley pulls me off this post and sends me down
there. They've started this new policy of skin-shaking the
dope fiends after their visits. You know what I had to do
yesterday?"

His face flushes. "I had to go through all this guy's
clothing, from the sweaty socks and shoes, go through the
lining of his shorts, the inside of his shirt and the lining of
his trousers. Then I had to start on this guy's body . . . this
meant the *entire* body! The armpits, spread his cheeks so I
could look up there, into his ears, his mouth, run my hands
through his hair, have him raise his balls to make sure he
had nothing hidden there."

He stops for a minute, looks down the corridor.

"You know what the goddamn Bothley did? He had
been standing behind me, supervising me! He stepped up
and said, 'Wait a minute, Galsworth, I don't think you're
interested in this job.' And he told the man to raise his
balls higher and bend back so he could see under there
better. Then he stepped back, looked at me as if to say,
'That's the way to do the job,' and walked away. Jesus
Christ, Charlie, sometimes I think there's something wrong
with that guy! I'm sure he went from there up to the
Personnel Office and put a memo in my folder."

I listen carefully, and only feel relieved that I went to
college and have the title of Counselor, which does not
require me to get involved in that kind of thing. Although,
theoretically, I suppose, if the need was there, I could be
forced to get involved; but in practice, it is never done. It's
like when a man escapes. Supposedly every available free
man in the prison is required to go out and search for him.
During an escape the atmosphere becomes charged with
excitement, practically everyone is issued a hand gun or a

rifle, the cars are readied, the local police are alerted, and the chase is on! Even if the escapee is an insignificant little alcoholic check-writer, impulsive enough to get himself rearrested immediately, anyway.

I know of at least one associate warden in the system who has left express orders that he is always to be informed, even if he is away on vacation, whenever there is an escape. As soon as he hears of an escape, he runs home (he lives on the grounds) and changes into tall leather boots, large Western hat, leather jacket, and completes the regalia with a riding crop—along with his heavy holster and gun, of course. And then, for him, the fun begins. I would love to talk with him about some of the feelings he has while tracking a man down. Naturally I suspect the obvious, a degree of sexuality involved. But then I guess there is that element in all prison work anyway, though few of us will admit it.

Though already disillusioned so early this morning, I try to appear interested in John's problem. "Something must have happened," I said, "for the administration to tighten things up."

He shrugs his shoulders. "Well, I guess so! The visiting room officer caught some guy's old lady giving him some stuff. Before they had a chance to nab him, he swallowed it. Didn't you hear about it? It happened about three weeks ago."

I shake my head.

"They took him to one of the administration offices, where they knew he couldn't contact another inmate, and kept him waiting there until he had to have a bowel movement. After a day and a half, with two officers on constant guard, he finally asked to go to the bathroom. They called Lieutenant Chuvalo, who had the guy crap onto a newspaper. The balloon came out all right, only before they could do anything, the guy swooped down, grabbed a hold of it and swallowed it again! You can imagine the looks on their faces! Only the guy didn't have a chance. Finally when he had to crap again, he gave up and just let them have it. Although he didn't struggle, they held him the second time. One of the officers had to dig in the guy's crap and come up with the balloon. After they'd washed it off, Chuvalo took it. But the thing that sickened me more than the incident itself, though that was bad enough, was the way some of the officers acted like Sherlock Holmes. You know, going around importantly, showing how smart they were, how they were finally able to get enough evidence on somebody so they could nail him in court.

"I don't know, Charlie, maybe this is too much for me. I've decided to try to get another assignment. Who knows, maybe I'm not cut out for this work. Maybe I just ought to quit and sell ice cream, or something."

He looks at me—desperately, I think—and goes on, "Anyway, I'd like to meet you for a drink after work and maybe get a little free therapy."

"Sure, John, I'll meet you down at the Hideaway in town."

After he lets me in the gate, I go to the top of the stairs and nod as an old officer, ex-Navy retired, lets me through a second gate leading to my office. As I enter, somehow it no longer seems to fit the description of a magic room where people are cured.

Chapter 2

The
Con

DUNN:

When I got up this morning, I noticed a ducat had been slipped under my door. Ducats for the next day are distributed by the first watch during the night. It was the regular kind of ducat, the penitentiary passport. If you're in a part of the joint where you usually have no legitimate business, you'd better have a ducat to be there, because somebody's sure to ask to see it, and without it you're dead. They are manila in color, two inches wide by three inches long, with printed instructions and spaces for the inmate's name, number, and destination, and they come in two parts. The top half, which is filled out by the Custody Office, is given to the inmate. The other half, which is torn off at its perforated edge, is kept for the Custody Office record. The ducats which are issued at night for the next day have to be turned in the following evening and compared with the other half on file to make sure that the convict reached the destination they wanted him to.

My ducat told me that Murray, the unit counselor, wanted to see me in his office. I wondered what the fool wanted, but could get no clue from thinking back on the way he has treated me lately or in the fact that the ducat was for 9:30 A.M., which is just after the group meeting. I assumed it must be something important because he hasn't had too much to say to me other than his usual jibes about when am I going to do something about myself. Each time he does that, I look at him like I don't know what he's talking about. But I always know what the idiot means. The thing is, he doesn't know I like things the way they are. He always comes on so mysterious as though he has a secret that I don't know. It's almost as though he's trying to entice me to find out what his secret is. But I already know what his secret is: he just plays his game. I know he wants to get into my melon and make a square out of me like he is. But I want no part of it. I'll let him go on and play his funny little game, because somehow I think he gets a kick out of it. But I'm hip to him, and I can beat him at it. If he wants to be mysterious with me, that's his business, but I know he's not going to know anything that I'm doing or thinking or planning to do. I'll give him the responses he wants each time he asks me something, but they'll never have anything to do with the way things are.

*   *   *

After the group meeting, I kill fifteen or twenty minutes
having a cup of coffee with Tommy. I'm almost getting used
to this instant coffee made with hot water in an old coffee
jar and drunk as though it were good. Coffee in the joint is
a big thing, the second biggest thing to cigarettes. It's a
ritual here; coffee jars come out of nowhere at the least
indication of a break in the routine or structure.

Because I'm never late for a ducat, or for anything, for
that matter, I leave early. I obey all rules in the penitentiary. It's the smart thing to do. As long as you don't give
them a chance to say anything to you, you're all right. At
9:25, I hike down the hall to the upstairs grill gate that
leads off the corridor just across from the mess hall and
above the Custody Office. The bull at the downstairs
station checks my ducat and unlocks the grill gate for me.
When I get to the top of the stairs, the bull at the other
grill gate has me pass my ducat through to him, reads it,
gets my I.D. card with its picture to make sure I am the
one who is supposed to pass, and unlocks the gate for me
to come into the inner sanctuary of the quack staff they
have here. After the bull lets me inside, he has me empty
my pockets on a table and assume the shakedown position:
legs spread and arms held horizontal from the body. Then
he begins the familiar shakedown. He starts at the nape of
my neck, feeling the seams of the collar, runs his hands
down my neck and over my chest, making sure to feel
under my armpits, and runs his hands down to my belt.
Then he runs his hands inside my belt to make sure I
haven't a weapon there. Next he briskly and efficiently
runs his hands over my buttocks and back pockets, then
around to my front pockets and joins both hands around
my leg and runs his hands down first one, then the other
leg to the shoe tops. He makes certain to feel the cuffs of
the trousers. At least he doesn't make me take off my

shoes and socks, as some of the bulls do. Then he tells me to go sit down on the bench along the side of the wall facing the offices.

The hallway is dull and cheerless, and I am alone sitting there. Apparently none of the other counselors had ducated anyone for this hour. I sit there for five minutes, and because Murray's door is open, I decide to stick my head in and let him know I am here. Murray's a funny-looking duck, right out of the prototype for Joe Square. He's average height, dark, thirty-six, and I heard he's never been married. I'm really suspicious of the bastard, and I know there's got to be something wrong with him. I can't help thinking to myself: "What's a guy doing spending his life in one of these shithouses when he could be doing something else?"

He's seated behind his desk, like all of these assholes are always seated behind their desks. For whatever reason, they need the protection of a desk. I guess it tells them who they are; having a desk lets them know they're big men. Actually, it's a small cubicle of an office, and I don't know how anybody could feel like a big man when all they can see out of their window is the cellblock opposite. But, I'm sure the stenotype recorder on his desk reinforces his image. He also has a few books on his desk which I suppose also makes him a big man, but the only book I really recognize is a copy of *The Penal Code*, one that I have good reason to know on sight. Papers are scattered all over his desk and this, too, I suppose is meant to give the impression of a busy and important man.

"You sent for me?"

"Yes, Jimmy," he says. "Have a seat. How've you been doing?"

He always gives me this bullshit, as if he cares how in the hell I've been doing.

"I'm all right."

"Well, I have some news for you. How do you feel about this?"

He hands me a legal-looking document and asks me to sit down. I open it and it's a petition and complaint, Dunn versus Dunn. That damn broad is divorcing me! The first thing I can think is, "That lousy bitch, wait 'til I get out of here and get my hands on that no-good, split-tailed animal, I'll beat her goddamn head in!"

The only reason I married her in the first place was because I knew I was coming back to the penitentiary. Sometimes the authorities won't authorize loose, stray broads for your mailing and visiting approvals, but they can't refuse you if you're married. I was going to need her to see me through this jolt, take care of my commissary money, visit, and what have you, so I married her.

The stinkin' animal, she knows she's got me down so she's going to kick me a little while I can't do anything about it! I wonder what in the hell got into her mind that she's brave enough to do this? I can't understand it, she knows me well enough to know I'm going to do something and she must know that it's going to mean lumps on her head.

A broad like that, kicking *me* when I'm down! I made her everything she is. She was just a dumb-ass college student when I got her and made her the best whore in town. She was top girl in every spot she worked, and she knows she's supposed to take care of me while I'm down. I made sure that I taught her that much. A good pimp doesn't care if a broad blows him while he's on the streets; it's part of the game. The world's full of broads, miss one streetcar, and four more come along, no problem. But this broad was with me two years, and I made her my main old lady. She knows she's supposed to take care of me now that I can't take care of myself. Goddamn, stinkin' snake, wait 'til I get my hands on her!

"Oh yeah, in a way, I was expecting it," I say. "I'm here for a while and a woman needs a man." This is the only thing he'll understand.

Then he gives me the stereotyped, case-worker pitch: "What do you think led to the divorce?"

I don't answer. Just look at him and shrug my shoulders. He's not satisfied, as I know he won't be, and begins his digging. "Tell me a little bit about the marriage."

I watch him for a few seconds, with the expression I use for these assholes, and come up with, "There's not much to tell."

True to form the hoosier next asks, "Early in the marriage, had you planned any children?"

Planned any children? Jesus Christ, this fool's too much! But this gives me the clue the idiot knows even less than I thought he did. I suspected they knew more about her and that it might be a matter of record that she's a whore. But this tells me they don't know anything about me or the whore. The police know. They've watched my house, and tailed the broad enough to know her action. It's a good thing the city bulls are hot at the state corrections and give them as little information and cooperation as they possibly can. The city police departments think that corrections is too easy on convicts and lets them back out too soon. And they seem to be more angry at corrections than they are at the convicts!

So I go along with Murray's game, because this, too, is what's expected of me. "No, I wasn't working. My wife was, but we didn't have enough money."

That's a laugh! I wasn't working, all right. She sure was! Bringing in that hundred to a hundred and a half every night. Top girl in every joint she worked! When I'm on the streets, I can buy and sell everyone of these hoosiers working here any day of the week. He can sit there and give me that square-ass bullshit of his. But I go along with it because that's the name of the game.

He flips through my file to refresh his memory. They must all look alike after a while. I see him stop at the yellow sheets, which I know are the cumsum (cumulative summary). I know he's going over my beefs, and getting clear in his mind what I've done and what I'm here for.

"I see in going over your file that at least you didn't repeat the same mistake twice."

I guess he's talking about the fact that the first time I was here was on a forgery beef and this time it's burglary.

"They were both accidents."

He looks up at me a little startled. "What do you mean by that? If you think the forgery was a mistake, what about the parole failure? Don't you think you belong here?"

"Oh, yeah, I committed the crimes, all right, but I was just in the wrong place at the wrong time."

He looks at me incredulously for a moment, and then I'm not sure what he's thinking. He looks almost as if he were angry. The damn fool, if he asks foolish questions, what does he expect but goddamn foolish answers?

Then he terminates the interview, I guess because he's not getting much information, and asks, "Have you got your ducat with you?"

"Oh, yeah, I'm sorry, I forgot it."

I hand him the ducat and he writes on the back of it the time I arrived and looks at his watch and writes the time I am leaving and underscores it with his initials. He hands the ducat back to me, and I'll have to turn it over to my crew-boss at vocational welding, so he'll know where I've been and why I'm late in arriving on the job.

"All right, Dunn, that'll be all; I'll see you around the wing."

"All right, Mr. Murray. Thanks a lot for seeing me and letting me know about this."

The

Interview

MURRAY:

Another bad group meeting. Every time I sit in a bad group, it ruins my whole day. Especially since the damn things are at 8:00 A.M. All we heard were the usual gripes about food, poor recreational facilities, not enough visits, shortage of clothing, and the lousy way the cellblock officer treats the men. As if that had anything to do with anything! But the men are captives, here against their will, with no reason to buy into the goals of the group or the prison system, except to manipulate it for their own ends.

At least I have the interview with Dunn to look forward to; maybe he'll brighten things up. Guys like Dunn make prison work interesting. You never quite know where you're at with them because they're so busy making you feel good. They actually succeed in persuading you that you are doing a worthwhile job.

Some guys seem to respond better in an individual interview than in group. Maybe I'm just going for a con that the inmates are putting on me. Maybe they are sincere and can't expose themselves in group for fear of being embarrassed, especially if it's a touchy personal problem. Maybe it's simply that I'm more comfortable in an individual interview. Usually I get the feeling that the inmate is listening intently to what I have to say. Of course, the intimacy of the situation tends to make me feel I'm really helping someone.

Even in an individual interview, it's difficult to work with a guy like Dunn because the system really doesn't allow him to change. In fact, the system will see to it that Dunn has little chance of changing. He knows the system and the system knows him. He is an efficient worker who gets top work grades. The minute he walks through the gate, no matter how many times he comes here, immediately he becomes part of the system, and his individual failure assures the success of the prison.

*   *   *

On the way back from the group meeting, held where the men live—in the five-hundred man cellblock that I'm responsible for—I pick up Dunn's file from the Record Office. I am reading it when he sticks his head around the doorway and says, "You sent for me?"

"Yes, Jimmy, come on in and have a seat. You startled me; I was thinking about something else."

Dunn takes the chair by the side of my desk. I keep it at the side rather than in front because I feel it reduces barriers between me and the inmate. Dunn flashes his usual, charming smile and makes himself comfortable by propping his elbow barely an inch away from the upright copies of the two "bibles" kept on the desk for constant reference: *The Penal Code* and *The Welfare and Institutions Code.* In sharp contrast, next to them are two books on group therapy.

"How have you been doing, Jimmy?"

In a way it's a ridiculous question. He has plenty of goodies from the canteen, chocolate bars, cigarettes, shaving creams, lotions, and sweet-smelling soaps. His old lady sends him $25.00 per month, the canteen limit. He can be taken care of sexually by one of the "queens" if he wants to, but I've never heard anything about Dunn on that score.

"I'm all right," he replies.

"I have some news for you. How do you feel about this?"

I hand him the familiar legal papers. There is no change of expression on his face. "Yeah, I was expecting it. I'm going to be here for awhile and a woman needs a man."

He's taking it rather lightly. It makes me wonder what that relationship was really about.

"What do you think led to the divorce?"

They were married shortly after he made parole on his first major incarceration. He was twenty-three; she was twenty.

When Dunn responds with a noncommital answer, I ask, "Tell me a little about the marriage."

"There's not much to tell." Cautious, suspicious.

"Early in the marriage, had you planned any children?"

No expression. I wonder what he really thinks about all this?

"No, I wasn't working, we couldn't afford it. My wife was, but we didn't have any money."

I can see this isn't getting anywhere and decide to take another tack. I flip his file over to the yellow sheets, the quick reference synopsis, and read the criminal history: a lot of arrests, but only two major convictions. The first was for forgery, this one for burglary, with an additional parole violation on the former.

"I see you didn't make the same mistake twice."

He smiles. "They were both accidents."

Suddenly I become irritated.

"What do you mean by that? If you think the forgery was a mistake, what about the parole failure? I suppose you think the parole agent was out to get you, and you really shouldn't have been violated?"

The parole report shows that Dunn had gone out to a nonexistent job, that he had not worked since the day he was released. For that matter, he had never worked a day in his life. It further reports that he always seemed to have plenty of money, nice clothes, and a nice place to stay. The parole agent could only report the facts as he discovered them. The wife was supposed to be working as a private secretary to a business representative, and she made many trips with him out of town. The whole thing seemed very mysterious. Naturally, the parole agent became suspicious, but matters were taken out of his hands when Dunn was picked up. Two alert police officers spotted him parked in the deserted plaza of a shopping district. Burglary tools were found in the car, and, on further investigation, it was found that the drug store in the plaza had been entered from the roof. A burglary conviction was obtained, even though nothing from the store was found in Dunn's car, and to the owner's best inventory, it couldn't be determined if anything was missing. Nevertheless, the circumstantial evidence was convincing.

"I committed the crime, all right," he replies with a wearied expression.

I'm not sure what this tacit admission of guilt means. It can merely mean that Dunn knows the Parole Board doesn't parole "innocent" men. Each man has to admit to the crime for which he was convicted before he's eligible for parole. If one doesn't admit his crime, the Parole Board takes the stand that since it's a matter for the courts to determine guilt, the Board, therefore, can't make a decision regarding parole. As far as the Parole Board is concerned, there aren't any innocent men in prison.

"Are you just saying that because you think that's what I want to hear? I see in your file that when you first returned, you had an appeal going. Don't you think you are really guilty?"

He gives that slow smile of his again and says, "I was just in the wrong place at the wrong time."

I become angry again, but try not to show it. Perhaps it's not even so much Dunn's fault as it is the system's. But there is nothing more to do with him this morning.

"Let me have your ducat, Jimmy, and you can go back to work."

"Thanks a lot for seeing, me, Mr. Murray," he says as he takes his signed ducat back. "It means a lot to have someone to talk to once in a while."

Dunn again flashes his charming smile and leaves.

I expected something more from him. Somehow guys like this are never really guilty. They're just a little guilty, like the girl who's a little pregnant. But once they get into the system, they run it for us and so are not entirely useless. They provide thousands of jobs for staff, including those who work for social agencies which give financial assistance to men's families. But nobody dares to change things and upset the status quo. For economic reasons if for no other, the prison system must be maintained. Consequently, the system doesn't want an examination of behavior, neither theirs nor the men's.

Take Dunn's divorce for example. If he had done some thinking about the kind of girl he was marrying at the time he married her—right after he'd gotten out on parole—he had no steady job, no money, and, in effect, not much to offer any girl, he should have been able to see that he was setting up failure for himself. In the first place, what type of girl would marry into those circumstances? Obviously she's either a "savior" or a masochist. But what really makes one wonder is what it is about this guy that makes him want to come to prison? I don't get it! A twenty-four-year-old, strong, healthy, good-looking, intelligent man who could easily go places and do almost anything! Instead, this is the life he chooses for himself. And before the Board lets him go again, he's going to have to do the time and come up with the magic set of words that will make them think he's going straight. But if he says anything wrong in his five- or ten-minute interview with them, or scares them in any way, he'll do at least an additional year. A whole year because you might scare one member of the Board or you might just, for instance, have a contemptuous attitude toward going to church on Sunday!

Actually the Parole Board does have a tough job. Some of the members are big on trades, others on education, and still others on church or group activity. The trouble comes when an inmate doesn't fit the particular Board member's expectations. I remember one inmate, Jack Gaines, who had that "hard" look about him. Jack was from Chicago, arrested on a trip out to the West Coast. He had been in trouble previously and was a product of the Illinois reform school. When we got him, he went through the "magic" group process. Jack was one of the exceptions. After a period of time in group, he really began to understand some of the reasons why he kept getting into trouble. But, unfortunately, this didn't do him much good at the Board. Jack got five years for armed robbery, his first adult offense. Usually the armed robbery average is three and a half years. As I remember the case, Jack didn't give the right answers and he angered the Board members with his sophisticated manner. He was a Roman Catholic, but stated he hadn't been in church for years and saw no reason why he should suddenly start attending simply because he was in prison.

*   *   *

Anyway, my desk looks as though I have enough paper work for a hundred years. If it's not letters to parents or wives, explaining why their males have been denied by the Board, it's responses to public agencies such as the District Attorney's Office, or the police, who have their own reasons for wanting to keep a certain man locked up.

Old man Brown is a good example. Thirty years ago, at the board meeting of a large department store chain, of which he was one of the principal directors, he shotgunned the entire eight-member board to death. He wiped them out. He has since been locked up. In the meantime, he's done a real service for us by reorganizing the psychology department and now knows more about projective testing than any two Ph.D.'s put together. Each year he goes before the Parole Board and each year he is denied. The Board appearance is almost a ritual. Because of the pressure to keep him in, the soruce of which is not known to me, the old man will probably die here. He keeps an orange crate full of letters he's received from the family survivors of the shooting, asking for his release, and regularly presents them to the Board. It's a pathetic scene, as he jealously protects his letters; but to date they've done him little good.

What possible good would it do Brown to have an individual interview with his counselor? I could interview him every day for the next five years, and he'll still never get out. So my choice is either Dunn or Brown, and I really can't know with any kind of certainty which will have the most effect.

The
Red Tape

DUNN:

"What are you doing here, Jimmy? Welding shop too much for you?" Fat Paul asks me as I come wheeling into the Custody Office from the main hall.

"No, man," I say. "I love the welding shop! I'm just here because Murray sent for me."

"Yeah, you're just here because Murray sent for you. I've seen all those requests for a job change. They must be killing you in that welding shop."

"Well, we'll see what I can do with them. What kind of mood are they in?" I ask, gesturing toward the classification offices. "Am I going to have to wrestle with them or are they going to give me a job change?"

"The only one I talked to before classification was Lieutenant Chuvalo," Paul answers, "and you know how that shithead is—the turd wouldn't give his mother a break. But hell, you know you got to fight him anyway. Your best bet is to work on Small; he's the biggest patsy."

I hand Paul my ducat—he'll take care of it for me and I won't have to talk to the bull. He'll have the control sergeant sign it and give it back to me when I come out.

Paul's a good man, a good convict—he knows the game and plays by all the rules. It's great to have a connection like Paul in the Custody Offices; he can keep us knowing what the enemy is doing.

We call him Fat Paul because when he's in the joint he puts on weight. On the streets he's a dope fiend and skinny as a rail. But everyone continues to call him Fat Paul. Even the narcotic and vice bulls know him as Fat Paul. He's a good-looking kid with a lot on the ball and a damn good pimp. Generally he's got good action on the streets, and he's a well-respected guy. He's had a little bad luck the last few years and he's now on his second jolt.

The Custody Office branches off from the main corridor. Control is on the right as you come in. Control is what the bulls call the nerve center of the prison. I guess they don't know the convicts couldn't care less what goes on in there. But anyway, there's always a sergeant on duty who is responsible for, and has to know all of the movement, and the whereabouts of every individual—both convict and guard—in the prison at all times. They keep all the extra sets of keys there and the rest of the ridiculous junk• that guards surround themselves with. Like I said, it's a great place to the bulls, and they get very upset when Control gets on their ass when the count isn't straight, but I couldn't care less what they do in there as long as they don't mess with me.

To the left of Control are the Custody Offices of the lieutenants with a small corridor between. At the back of this area is a large conference room where they have classification and disciplinary meetings. There's a small waiting room with benches along the walls in front of the conference room. The whole area is painted a lemon yellow. Paul's desk is in front of the first office of the Custody section, and he sits in there all day (and I don't know how he can stand it!) with the correctional officer who is the day-watch control officer.

After leaving Paul's office, I walk down the passageway to find six other guys seated on the benches waiting to go to classification. I don't know any of them. They're just more of the penitentiary hoosiers who are always around. I sit down on one of the benches which is empty and act as though I don't see the other guys seated there.

But I see them all right. Typical jailhouse hoosiers. You can see they're scared—afraid because they have to face the Man. One of them is seated, bent over with his elbows on his knees and his hands clasped in front of him. His knuckles are white with the tension, he's so scared. "Goddamn," I think, "if he can't face classification in the penitentiary, how in the hell does the hoosier feed himself on the streets?" That's probably why he's here, because he can't feed himself on the streets; as bad as the chuck is here, at least it's more regular for some people.

The rest of the guys are just sitting around, acting like it's not a big thing. But I know it's a big thing, because I'm even a little anxious myself. I've got to get out of that welding shop! I still can't understand how the hell I got in there in the first place. I just happened to hit initial classification at the wrong time. Of course, initial classification is always the worst. When you first come in, they assign you to a job. You always get the worst jobs in the joint. It's because they can't give them to the older cons who have been there awhile, so the "fish" get stuck with them. It was just my snake-bitten luck that they needed guys in the welding shop to fill up their quota for "vocational training" when I went to classification. Of course, I knew all about the welding shop from the last time, but they wouldn't let me talk my way out of it. But I know I've got to get out of there now! Goddamn! Me in welding shop? That's really ridiculous!

The buzzer over the door sounds, and the hand-wringer jumps up as though he's been shot and rushes into the classification office. I can't help thinking to myself, "I wonder who he's going to snitch on in there?" He looks so weak I can't see him making it out of the penitentiary any other way than by snitching his way out.

Five minutes later, he comes out again with a dazed look on his face. Only one of two things could have happened, I think, as he walks down the corridor to get his pass in Paul's office. Either he got what he wanted and it shocked him, or he didn't get what he thought he deserved and he can't understand how the officials can be so stupid as not to recognize what a fine guy he is.

One by one the other five guys go into the room at the sound of the buzzer and come out again. I know I am next. We all know the rules. You don't have to be very smart in order to know that when you come into a room and everybody there is supposed to go into the inner office, that you can't look around and see who is there before you in order to know what your position on the list will be. In fact, you get trained here pretty good; just like Pavlov's dog, you'll respond to buzzers, bells, and lights, and whatever else they give you.

I am beginning to get even more nervous when they take so long after the last guy comes out, but finally the buzzer sounds again and I go in. Six familiar faces are seated around a big conference table. The room is bare, with two high windows, barred, of course, at the far end. Otherwise, there are just the tables and chairs and six bored-looking faces as I walk in. Murray, seated at the head of the table, as my counselor, will present my case to the rest of the board. On his right is Lieutenant Chuvalo, and next to him on the same side of the table is Mr. Sansome. Dr. Palow is seated next to him. Across from Chuvalo, and on Murray's left, is Thompson. Next to him is Mr. Small, the supervising counselor, who is closest to me as I take the seat indicated at the foot of the table.

I take a quick look at Chuvalo, a small, chisel-face Mexican with a hard-on for the world. I know he's going to be trouble. His nut-brown face tells me nothing except that he doesn't like me. Mr. Sansome is a tall, slender, white-haired old guy with a booming voice who is generally pretty ineffectual. He'll be no problem. Thompson from Education is a tall, athletic-looking, bald-headed guy with an obsequious manner. I've already talked to him before, and he knows I want no part of him or the Education Department, so he won't be a problem, either. Like Fat Paul said, Small will be my best bet. Most of the guys treat him like a broad because he looks like one. And just like a broad, he cons easy.

Murray opens the meeting with his usually goofy manner by saying, "How come we're seeing you at the Classification Committee today?"

This damn idiot! He's constantly playing his little psychological games and thinks everybody's going to go for the bait. I've been talking to the hoosier for the past nine months, ever since I saw him at the interview about the divorce, about trying to get out of the goddamn welding

shop. He knows exactly why I'm here today. I go along
with the game like always, and give him the answer he
wants.

Just as I knew he would, the turd, Chuvalo, has to horn
in with his left-handed bullshit, "What are you doing now,
Dunn?"

I got to be careful with this asshole—he's nothing but
trouble. So, I play it cool with him; "I've been in welding
shop for the past nineteen months."

When I say that, Sansome perks his head up and takes a
look at me. He doesn't know me from a load of coal, but
that's his department we're talking about now, and you can
see that we've disturbed his sleeping place.

The patsy, Small, comes on in his usual social-worker
way, "Isn't your name Jimmy? Why do you want to
change, have you finished the course?"

I've got to be careful, I don't want to alienate my best
bet. If I'm going to do anything, it'll be with Small. "No,
but I want to be a hall porter." I know that sounds lame, so
I come up with something better for this guy. "Really, I
think it's a good job, and I could get along good there."

Old mealy-mouthed Thompson shows a little fight—I
guess that's how he's been able to get by all these years,
forcing himself to act the part he's not. But he makes like
the typical teacher, with his moralizing and nothing-bullshit
that I really don't want to hear.

"What's a porter's job prepare you for? You don't have a
trade, you don't have a high school diploma. In fact, the
way you are now, you're completely unskilled."

Jesus, I didn't expect any trouble from this whore.
"That's not true. I have a skill. I'm a bartender."

I don't like the way this meeting is going, it doesn't look
at all good. I wonder to myself, "What the hell's going on?
They're giving me the third degree about a goddamn hall

porter's job." I don't understand it. It's no big thing. They hand out these shuck jobs every day. I wonder what they're beefing me about?

Sansome gives me some more trouble about preparing myself for the outside world.

Oh, man! What are these whores doing? Are they going to give me the job or not?

I say something about how I'm going to be here for a long time, and immediately I know that it was the wrong thing to say. Just as soon as I said it, Chuvalo looks up quickly with that hard, baleful look he has for convicts.

"Then why do you want a porter's job? You want to wheel and deal?"

Just like always, he's trouble.

"No, that's not it; look at my institutional record, I've never had a beef. Porters are needed, that's all, and I'd like the job."

I look up at Murray, trying to get some help from him; after all, he's my counselor. It's supposed to be his job to help me. At least that's the shuck they give you.

But Murray's not going to give me any help, and he tries to close the meeting. "Well, you don't sound too convincing to me. I think you better go back to welding and complete the course. This will at least show some stability and maturity on your part."

Stability and maturity? Jesus Christ! The same tired words given in an unending repetition. I'm so sick of those two goddamn words I could puke every time I hear them. Stability and maturity. What the hell do they mean? These assholes are constantly using the terms but they don't ever bother to tell anyone what they mean. But I think I know what they mean. They mean if you have those things, then you're Joe Square. And if having maturity and stability means I'm going to have to be like these assholes, they then can keep them!

But I can see I'm in bad shape trying to get a job change out of these fools today. I still don't understand what the hell's happening. I'm not asking for a goddamn thing but a hall porter's job! What the hell are they making a federal case out of it for?

But I have to try them one more time.

"Wait a minute here. Before we just shut this off—don't do me like this. Look at it from my angle. What am I doing in welding? You're trying to make a welder out of me. The only reason I got there in the first place is because there wasn't anything else open when I went to initial classification. I don't even like welding! I'll never do anything with it."

Old Sansome, with his booming voice, probably because he's hard of hearing, tries to pacify me. He gives me some "con" about trying harder.

What's the matter with these people? Can't they look at me and see I would never be a welder?

"But look at it from my point again," I say. "How am I going to like something I just despise?"

Now even Murray begins to get after me. "What are you really trying to do with this porter's job, have a lot of free time?"

I really can't understand it. What's all this beef about? You'd think I asked them for a parole! The only thing I want is a goddamn porter's job.

"Well, what do the rest of you gentlemen think?" Murray asks after I've responded. He's trying to shut it off again.

Small answers, "Since there seems to be some confusion about what to do with this man, we'll postpone a decision for four weeks, and we'll hold another classification meeting at that time."

Small looks at me with that shit-eating smile of his as though to say, "Well, I've done you a favor; at least we didn't say no and you can come back in four weeks."

But I'm so damn hot by now that I know I had better get out of there before I say something. I don't even answer Small, but just get up and get the hell out before I really get myself into a jackpot. After going down the hall I stop in at Paul's office to pick up my ducat.

"What happened in there?" Paul asks, as he hands me the ducat.

"What the hell's going on around here," I answer. "Am I on some kind of list or something? Those bastards wouldn't give me anything."

"Look for me in the mess hall tonight, Jimmy," Paul says, "I'll check around and see what I can find out."

"O.K., Paul. Thanks. I'll see you."

But one thing I already know it means—for some reason, I am skating on thin ice around here. In some ways the group meeting might be useful. Maybe one of these staff whores would slip and I'd get an idea of what they plan to do with me.

The Policy-Makers

MURRAY:

Staff meeting, another problem! What the meeting boils down to is a group of staff getting together, each with his pet projects and vested interests, tugging at the raw material, the inmate, who is caught in the middle. The inmate becomes a gigantic human pie, with each staff member bidding for more of his time and wanting a larger slice. All the separate functions of the prison need bodies in order to function and survive.

Not only is this the way it operates here, but also throughout the entire department. Each institution, having

grown tremendously in the past few years, has a minimum
number of inmates which they consider necessary to operate their programs. The practice of fulfilling these obliga-
tions cloaks itself in the euphemism of "institutional
needs." It sometimes happens, because an inordinate number of paroles have been granted at any particular time
(this phenomenon sometimes has political overtones), that
an institution suddenly finds itself short of bodies. Panic
sets in. The institution in need informs the state capitol.
The bureaucratic machine then starts grinding.

Inmates who had previously requested, and had been
denied, transfer to a less custody-minded institution, sud-
deny find themselves prime transfer material. When the
dumbfounded inmate asks what he has done to warrant this
sudden change of institutional policy, he is merely told,
"Institutional needs." Also, this is the way it appears on all
official records. Consequently, what is "policy" today may
be something else tomorrow, without regard to what is
most appropriate for the inmate.

We generally hold staff meetings and classification meetings in the conference room at the rear of the Control and
Custody Offices. The room is well appointed, furnished
with a rich-looking boardroom table and eight comfortable
leather chairs. The walls are panelled in mahogany. It is
fairly quiet, except for the noise which sometimes filters
through the two high, barred windows from the inmates
outside. If we had ever listened carefully, perhaps we might
get some real understanding of the inmate world. But,
unfortunately, we're too busy to listen. We have an institution to run!

When I walk into the conference room, the only one
there is Fred Thompson, doctorate in Education (Teachers'
College, Columbia). Erudite, suave, loves fine food and
good wine. Enjoys long vacations and climbing mountains

with his wife and three kids. He drives a Porsche and naturally lives in the nearby upper-middle-class community.

"Hi, Fred. Ready for another meeting of the minds?"

"You know me, Charlie," he responds, "I enjoy our weekly verbal contests."

Even Custody is less rigid than these school people. They operate under the premise that education is the best method of keeping men out of prison. Their policy consists of giving the inmates plenty of educational and vocational training. In this method Thompson has a ready ally in Gordon Sansome, supervisor of vocational trades. Give the men a high school diploma and a trade, and they'll never commit another crime. Only they've tried it for years now and it hasn't worked out.

I no more than take my seat when the rest of the assigned staff begin arriving. Sansome is the first to come in, followed by Louis Palow, M.D., chief psychiatrist. Then Lieutenant Chuvalo, Custody (I never did get to know his first name, because he always introduced himself as "Lieutenant"). Edward Small, supervising counselor, and William Chase, the associate warden, follow. The latter, in the best of parliamentary traditions, will conduct the meeting.

Chase opens by saying, "Last week we ended the staff meeting by coming to some understanding of the problems of this institution."

"Bumbling Bill" the inmates had aptly nicknamed him. As innocuous as that opening statement is meant to be, it sets off something in Fred Thompson. He reacts immediately.

"I'm glad you think there was some understanding," he challenges. "As far as I'm concerned, this damn group therapy program you have going is upsetting my entire school program. The men are always straggling in, and the teachers are kept waiting. If the inmates want to go to group, they should go to group, but not on school time. If they want an education, they should be in school."

Small, my supervisor, jumps right in. "I don't see how you can make that sharp a division, Fred. It seems to me we have people here ill-equipped educationally, vocationally, and emotionally. Even if we work cooperatively together, we barely have time to meet all of these needs."

Fred is sizzling by now.

"In order to maintain my budget on an annual basis," he says, "I have to have so many pupils in each class. You gentlemen seem to forget that we're operating on the average-daily-attendance principle for financing. I can't get the budget I need to maintain the program when men are absent. If this keeps up I'll have to let a teacher go. This would reduce the number of courses we are able to offer the men. How are they going to get the benefits of a well-rounded high school education without enough teachers?"

He goes on, hardly pausing for breath, "I feel that some changes could be made by the treatment staff. Why don't you people have your groups at night?"

I glance at Bumbling Bill, who is already uncomfortable. There is no denying he has a deep interest in the welfare of the men, but he also can't handle staff differences, particularly an open breach between departments. I know it is very difficult for him to take a stand unless he is really pushed up against the wall, especially if he feels personally threatened.

Bill tries to play peacemaker.

"It seems to me," he says, "we should take a clearer look at the issues. We should have more open communication and work out some of our problems, rather than have sharp ultimata."

He turns toward Ed Small and goes on, "Would it be possible to end the group meetings five or ten minutes earlier so that the men would have more time to walk to the shops and classrooms?"

Small tries to explain. "That would not be possible. Besides, it really wouldn't help. We have some of the vocational instructors in the groups as coleaders, and we like them to stay with us following the group for a fifteen-minute postsession."

Ed waits for a reaction for a second, but then apparently thinks better of it, and before he can get one, pushes his point farther. "Each staff member, in our setting, is an integral part of a large therapeutic community. We like to know what they think they heard in a total unit meeting, how it affected them, and then to have a discussion about their own participation. As it stands now, the postsessions have been cut down from a half-hour to fifteen minutes, and I feel this was a major concession. I also feel this is the only time we get a chance to examine the role of each staff member in a group so that he can validate some of the things the men say about educational or vocational matters."

That last bit is really a bouquet to the school people in an attempt to appease them. He knows that the men spend very little time discussing these topics.

As he always does, Chuvalo takes the part of the educational-vocational combine. They are less threatening to Custody's authority. He always protects his own interests; in fact, he is more concerned about his own welfare than that of the inmates. I guess ambition, and the way he's chosen to get ahead, partly explains it. He's a thirty-five year old Mexican-American who has found acceptance in Civil Service. A high school graduate, he has been enrolled at the local State College for the past six years, slowly

working toward his Bachelor's degree. When he finally gets
it, he will have more ammunition for his next promotion.
Although he realizes the promotional necessity of a college
degree, he really doesn't believe that he will learn anything
which will help him deal with the men. Custody is sure
they know the men. Chuvalo is highly suspicious of inmates, and more so of staff who try to make changes in
the existing program.

"I think," he says, "the running of the institution comes
first. We have a lot of work to do, and the work program
should not be cut down just for the sake of therapy
groups. What these guys need more than anything is good
work habits, just like anybody else. I don't really see the
value of babying them and putting them in group every day
so we can go through some crazy psycho routine of trying
to find out 'why' they commit crimes. Who cares whether
they want to sleep with their mother or sister and have
'*underlying hostilities*'?"

That last is said with a sneer. He is obviously pleased
with himself at using some of our own professional jargon
he has picked up at college. He seems to be warming to the
subject and thoroughly enjoying himself.

"What these guys need," he continues, "is to be taught a
lesson, and the only way we can do this is to see that they
work every day, go to school, and try to make something
of themselves. I don't think we ought to let them get away
with the excuses they come up with for committing crimes.
If we do, they'll just go out and start all over again. *We*
have to work for a living, and I think these guys ought to
be taught something about responsibility."

He settles back in his chair waiting for some reaction
from the rest of us.

"I don't think there is any proof that any of the things
we've tried so far is especially effective," I say, hoping to

turn the meeting another way. "It seems to me we're groping in the dark. For years we tried corporal punishment. That didn't work, but still some states and some of the prisons in our own system use it, though officially we won't admit it. All the treatment staff is really asking is for some of the men's time. We feel that with this we can begin a dialogue, probably for the first time in the inmates' lives, relative to holding them accountable for their behavior. I don't think, as some of the staff obviously do, that we are preaching the need for deep therapy, or that every inmate should have a couch and be psychoanalyzed, or that we should examine his early toilet training. But I do think it is unrealistic to assume just because we raise his grade level three or four notches, or he gets the fundamentals of a trade, that he is therefore going to stay out of trouble. If we get stuck in either situation, we're more naive than I think we are."

"Murray, you think that all you have to do is talk about something and it makes it so." Sansome is angry as he responds to my comments. I touched a sensitive area. Basically Sansome is a good craftsman and a decent supervisor for his vocational teachers. But he does not want anyone to mess with his private world. He loves nothing better than to take visitors to the prison around the shop areas and show them the expensive electronic equipment, or the highly complex aerodynamics area, where only a handful of inmates—due to the lack of math training—could qualify. There's no denying that men, if they're serious, can be trained well in prison. But at the same time, the sad thing is that the men who can qualify for these complex trades are the very ones who need the training the least. Moreover, the tremendous cost of these plant areas, in terms of return for each dollar spent, is prohibitive. In the meantime, for the most part, members of the minority groups who need the training the most are being kept in the status they have in the outside community: general laborers, agricultural workers, and janitors.

"I didn't say that, Gordon," I answer. "I simply mean that there is a little evidence to indicate that lack of a trade, or no high school diploma is the reason why people commit crimes. I think it's a little more complex than that. Part of our problem is to find out what it is. All we're asking for is some systematic daily program where the men can feel free to talk about themselves, knowing that what they say in group won't be held against them in some way. For example, if a guy sits in group and admits he's a child molester and tries to deal honestly with his behavior, we should be able, as a beginning, to demonstrate that we will not hold his past against him. But, that's only one of the problems. There are a number of others. I don't think the counseling staff should be undermined in what they are attempting to do."

Chuvalo jumps at that. "Now you're sounding as paranoid as the men." Again he seems pleased at being able to use the words of the trade. "What makes you think you guys are being undermined?"

"Well, I'll give you an example," I answer. "I don't think we should expect the inmates to do something that the staff is apparently reluctant to do. Many of the Custody and vocational people are consistently late coming to group meetings. If the treatment staff says to the inmates that groups are important, that we expect the men to be on time, it seems to me that the least we can expect is for the rest of the staff to also be there on time. I guess, though, there's another way around it, if that's what will be necessary. Maybe we should start grouping the staff in the large meeting about why they're late and not participating."

"You wouldn't dare." Dr. Palow finally breaks his silence. "I don't think it's wise for men to see a division or a breach between the different factions or departments."

He has a way of speaking which always makes me think of political contests.

"Well, Louis, that's precisely one example of our many problems," I say. "I think it's unrealistic for us to deceive ourselves that the men don't realize the staff can disagree. What's wrong with disagreement? The whole world disagrees. Is that a rule of institutions? Maybe that's the reason inmates keep coming back, because this is the only place in the world where everything is always the same. Why can't we share some of our problems with the inmates, Louis?"

He hates it when I call him Louis, or even worse, Louie, especially when others are present. He feels that as a psychiatrist he should always be addressed as Dr. Palow— not even just plain Doctor.

The first few weeks he was here, he wore a long, white coat while conducting interviews in his office. Maybe they still do that in Europe, where he was trained. At any rate, the white coat sure kept the inmates at a distance, although some were impressed and loved it. Finally, one day, the white coat disappeared. The story was that some inmate had stolen it. It was never found, and never replaced. Perhaps he felt it best to ignore it. Now he merely wears conservative business suits. Palow really knows nothing about groups. He is only part-time at the institution, and his main role is to decide when an inmate is sufficiently disturbed to be sent to the state medical facility. He only works here one day a week. The rest of the time he has a private practice in the Valley, mostly with middle- and upper-middle-class neurotics.

I feel he is a phony. But the department has something going about window dressing their institutions with psychiatrists in order to impress the public and the legislature. The budget calls for a psychiatrist, and each institution has one of the local men. I guess it's impressive when the brochures of a prison state that "psychiatric consulting services are available." It's like some kind of voodoo magic. The public gets the impression that every inmate gets psychiatric treatment and is, therefore, cured, or changed in some magical way.

I go on: "I didn't say we would do this. All I said was that it might be a good idea. We just might want to try it some day."

"I don't think the institutions are quite ready for that, at this time," he responds.

I am getting angry now. "I don't want to fall into that line of reasoning," I challenge. "In fact, I think administrators, and even some treatment people, feel there is something magical about being ready for a certain type of program. As far as I'm concerned, as long as the composition of the institution keeps changing, I don't see why we don't have some new programs. Men come and go and staff comes and goes. Somehow the programs seem to remain the same."

I can sense Sansome and Thompson getting ready for a dual attack.

"When my teachers came to work for the institution as vocational instructors," Sansome opens up, "they did not bargain to get involved in some new-fangled therapy program. In the first place, what can they be expected to know about groups. They're *educators* by training."

He stresses the word as if he is afraid nobody will believe him. He gets immediate support from Thompson.

"I feel the same way," Thompson says. "What do you counselors know about vocational work? I don't see the counselors in the vocational area working with the men. We don't expect you to work in our province; I don't see why we should be expected to work in your area of specialty. Or is it rather that you assume that anyone can do counseling or group work?"

At this point Small decides to give me some help. I guess he is angry too.

"No," he quickly says, "I don't think just anybody can be a group leader, if that's what you mean. It does take a certain acquired skill, but it assumes that the leader or coleader has had some living experiences he can call on in an effort to work with other human beings. After all, it's akin to a family where the father has more experiences than the other members of the family. The children look to the father for guidance and a certain kind of protection. I'm sure that many inmates see a number of us in the same role, whether we want to admit it or not. But the point I'd like to make is that we may as well capitalize on it and attempt to counsel them through the use of daily group meetings."

That is quite a bit coming from Small. To my knowledge, this is the first time he's expressed his ideas on the place of treatment in the prison so clearly in a staff meeting. He's been in the system long enough to be more of a politician than that!

Chuvalo begins to squirm in his seat.

"I'm nobody's daddy!" he explodes. "I have enough problems with my own family. I don't feel like playing daddy to any of these jokers!" (It is certainly true that Chuvalo has plenty of personal problems. He has been divorced twice and the rumor is that he is now running around with a married woman ten years his senior.) He has no close friends, but is friendly with everyone. He is even outwardly friendly with treatment people, though it certainly doesn't seem so today!

Bill Chase is getting more and more restless. He is chain-smoking now, a sure sign of his distress. He keeps looking at his watch and I know that he will shortly try to end the meeting.

Before anyone can respond to Chuvalo, Bill says, "Perhaps we had best postpone further discussion of this until next week. I realize we are making a great deal of headway into this particular problem; however, we do have a Classification Committee meeting scheduled for this hour, and I have a meeting with the I.R.C. right now. My schedule is too tight this morning to continue with this."

Poor Bill. He can't handle the staff differences so he uses the Inmate Representation Council as an excuse to break up the meeting. The I.R.C. is a group of con-wise, institutionalized, slick, and verbal inmates who have bamboozled the prison administrators in this state into believing that inmate representation is a necessary part of prison life. It's like a union. It has some of the attributes of an industrial union, bargaining for the inmate body, and is supposedly the voice of the inmate. Implicit in the idea of the I.R.C. is the message that if the inmate body isn't listened to, there will be trouble in the prison. The word "riot" is often carelessly thrown about and is calculated to frighten staff.

The original idea in back of the founding of the I.R.C. was a sound one. It was an attempt to find out how the men really felt about prison policies. In the best traditions of a democratic society, the administrators sought the assistance of the inmate leaders. But today the picture is quite different. The slick, manipulative inmates are using it for their exclusive gain. Being a member of the I.R.C. also looks good for the Parole Board. The staff, in return, uses the I.R.C. to suppress trouble in the institution, and it helps them to run a riotless, smooth institution—exactly what the public wants.

Bill Chase rises and says, while standing, "All right, gentlemen, we have to get on with the institution's business." He smiles in his pleasant, meaningless way and goes on, "I'll be getting on to the I.R.C. meeting now, but let's remember what took place this morning so we can continue next week."

Bill leaves the room while the remainder of us settle down to becoming the Classification Committee. It's strange how we assume that merely changing the name of our meeting from Staff to Classification will make it easier for us to, as Bill said, "get on with the business of the institution." The problems expressed this morning, especially since there was no resolution and anger was evident, will spill over on to the Classification Committee meeting, and, as usual, the inmates will get caught in the middle.

Lieutenant Chuvalo picks up the Conference Room telephone and calls the Record Office to have the girl bring in the files on the men who are to appear before the Classification Committee. At this interruption we all seem to relax a bit and light cigarettes. Normally we would break for coffee, but it will only take the girl a few minutes to wheel in the cart with the files and there isn't that much time.

Chuvalo settles back comfortably and gives me a pleasant smile.

"Been drinking any good wine lately, Charlie?" He often jokes with me about my taste for good wine and food. I think it's a mystery to him why anyone would spend more than two dollars on a bottle of wine.

"As a matter of fact," I answer, "I had an excellent bottle of Chateau Haute Brion '47, with dinner night before last. Too bad you weren't with me! I think you'd have enjoyed it."

He smiles. "I don't know whether I would or not. Unlike you counselors I have to work hard every day!"

Everyone laughs. Just at this moment, the door opens, and the file girl wheels in the cart with the morning's work.

The first six cases go rather routinely. For the most part, Chuvalo makes the decisions as they are all for reduction of custody. The lieutenant really enjoys that role. He feels much more comfortable with structure, with the specific criteria clearly spelled out. It's easy to make that kind of decision. The state has laid the rules out in the departmental classification manual. But the Classification Committee does have considerable leeway. It can completely disrupt an inmate's existence, for instance, by changing his job, taking him out of school or a trade, placing him in the Adjustment Center because of poor behavior, or sending him to another institution of higher or lower security. In some respects the Classification Committee is like the all-powerful judge, God, and father all rolled into one. Once a decision has been made, it cannot be changed, except by another order of the Classification Committee.

This next case would be a little different. Dunn, in whom I had taken a special interest since our interview about the divorce almost a year ago, is asking to be taken out of vocational welding, and I think some problems might arise.

Chuvalo hands me Dunn's file, an exceptionally thick one for so young a man. Life histories in prison can be measured by the thickness of files.

The lieutenant smiles at me: "What do you want us to do for your friend Dunn this morning?"

"I'm not sure," I answer, "but I think he's coming in for a job change."

Ed Small also appears interested. "I don't know Dunn too well; in fact, I'm not sure if many of us have any real knowledge of what changes Dunn's made since he's been here."

He is evidently giving me the lead and continues, "Why don't you give us a quick rundown, Charlie, on how he appears to you at this time?"

I know that many of the staff members are hostile toward Dunn, particularly the Custody staff, so I begin to give my perception of him as gently as I can.

"I see Jimmy Dunn as a smooth, sharp, twenty-four-year-old man who is extremely perceptive in pinpointing the weaknesses of other people and plays on those weaknesses."

I glance around at the other members to see how my first statement is being received. Everybody appears to be listening intently.

"He's the product of a broken home," I continue, "his mother and father having separated when he was two years old. From that time on he was handed around from one foster placement to another, school to school, agency to agency, and institution to institution."

I begin to forget about some of the frustration of the earlier staff meeting as I talk enthusiastically about Dunn.

When no one interrupts me, I go on, "Jimmy has been able to 'con' most people who have come into contact with him. If he is not able to do this, he drops them like hot potatoes. He has been badly hurt by what he sees as a total rejection from the world. In his life I doubt if he has ever trusted anyone."

As I say that, I glance over at Chuvalo, who has never trusted anyone either.

"We have here a person who does not learn from his own experiences, nor the experiences of others. He takes undue advantage of people who want to be taken advantage of. He does not appear to have any real conscience. He has shown poor judgment over and over again. He is unresponsive in most interpersonal relationships. He has a

great deal of charm, but little warmth to go with it.
Basically he is a very hostile person, and there will always
be the danger he might injure someone."

I know that a statement like this will stir many anxieties
in some of the staff members here, but I can't give a true
picture of Dunn without including it.

Still no one interrupts me.

"I don't think he would ever kill anyone; he's so rigid
that he does have some controls. He has no love for
women, which is the reason he treats them the way he
does. In all probability he would be homosexual, except he
cannot handle that kind of feeling. He is too busy telling
the world how masculine he is, which explains why he
spends so much time in keeping his body in trim while he's
in prison."

I look at Dr. Palow, whose expression is noncommital.

"If we were to take a Freudian view," I continue, "we
might say that Dunn is getting back at his mother for dying
by using women the way he does. He is basically a sadist;
not that he is always beating up on someone, merely that
he places the other person, especially women, in a groveling
position. He must be able to control and dominate women;
otherwise he drops them.

"For example, Dunn will put his women to work for
him on the streets so that he can purchase fine clothes,
cars, and generally lead the life of a wealthy playboy.
There isn't anything in his file to substantiate this. But as I
see it for this type of person, if the gal refuses to work for
him, he has several choices. He can either beat her up to
get her in line, or, if she is strong enough—or not sufficiently masochistic—and decides to leave him, he must look
around for another girl who *is* masochistic and wishes to be
dominated. Since there is no shortage of these women,
Dunn will lead a very active life, at least until he is about

fifty and loses some of his charm, or acquires a sizeable paunch to replace his slim waist. At that time his sexual energy will be reduced; even then I think he may still be attractive to certain women—after all, Don Juan was not exactly handsome."

No one asks any questions when I pause. I begin to wonder whether my description is too complicated, or whether the committee simply doesn't agree with me.

"Are there any questions so far?"

"You're doing fine, Charlie," Small says. "Why don't you continue."

However, Louis Palow stops me before I can. "What are the treatment prospects for a man like this in our prison system? What you have described is the classical psychopath."

I feel I am getting some support. "I agree, Louis, I do not feel we are set up to raise this man's anxiety, which is what we need to do. After all, why *should* he change? He knows the prison system like the palm of his hand, better than most staff members. He can do time standing on his head.

"What I suggest is that he would need to be placed in an institution with a true indeterminate-type sentence, one which would not base his release on whether he goes to church or not, or whether he has so many hours in a vocational trade which he won't make use of anyway. Our task with Dunn is to get him to face himself and really examine his behavior in such a way that it will make him uncomfortable. There is no change unless there is some emotional discomfort. Except for the first few days he is in an institution, I doubt that Dunn has ever had an uncomfortable day in prison. In fact, it may be that the prison is a kind of haven for him; that is, when the pressures get to be too great on the outside, he can manage things so that he will be caught and locked up. He knows that eventually he will be given his freedom and returned to society. When this happens he almost immediately gets involved again in delinquency. What we have here, in effect, is a guy who lives in two worlds. In the one he maintains the playboy image with the additional excitement of trying to outwit the police. In the other, he reenters the protective, womb-like atmosphere of the prison where he has his canteen privileges, gratis medical and dental attention (except for the two cartons of cigarettes to the inmate clerk for putting him on the waiting list), even a queen or two begging for his favors. Consequently, he is, even while in prison, able to enjoy most of the privileges of a free society. In reality, he may even manage to be more free in a prison than many of us are in a nonprison world.

"Dunn has learned to accept and to deal with some of the more difficult staff members. He operates in the typically sociopathic manner: he is doing one thing, and they think he is doing another. He is subservient to them when in their presence. This makes them feel good because they feel they're helping Dunn finally to make some changes in his life-style.

"In brief, we have here a young man we are not equipped to deal with in this kind of set-up."

When I finish I have the feeling that I have gone too far, especially with the last damning statement. There is absolutely no response. I look around at their faces, trying to get some clue as to what they might be thinking.

Chuvalo sits with clenched teeth, the sinews in his hard face showing clearly. Does this mean he doesn't believe my interpretation? Probably with his philosophy of custody control he thinks that given enough time, the system can break a guy like Dunn. But how does that explain the sixty-year-old, five-time-loser types exactly like Dunn who are walking around our prison yards? Sansome apparently didn't even hear what I said; he looks completely disinterested. Somehow I have the feeling that he can't reconcile his notions of vocational training with the picture I have just described. He believes that a good trade equals a good life. If Dunn can be taught a good trade, he would automatically be a good citizen, regardless of the psychological complexities. Thompson looks depressed. I know enough about him to know that when he came into prison work, after his own sacrifices for a Ph.D., it was with the idea of helping people. Now after fifteen years he is struck with the stark reality of having to work with hopeless cases. Ed Small is smiling. Pleased, no doubt, with my interpretation, because I know, from our many talks, that he agrees with me on some of the central problems in prison work. The only major difference between us is in implementation; he tends to be more traditional and conservative whereas I tend to be more aggressive in trying to make some changes. Palow looks pensive. I get the strange impression that perhaps he is thinking about recommending Dunn for shock treatment. I remember that the doctor was instrumental in setting up the electroshock therapy program here, which has degenerated into further tool for Custody. It is used on tough disciplinary cases—even the toughest con will become amenable to anything the staff wants after he gets enough of that juice.

Thompson finally breaks the silence and asks, "You've given us a lot of information about how you see Dunn, but what is the prognosis for his future?"

My answer is short and sweet. "The outlook for the future is grim. Unless Dunn can find a way to channel his excessive sexual energy, which drives him to antisocial behavior, I'm afraid we'll have him for a long time on the good old installment plan."

Chuvalo starts in slowly, "Listen, Murray, I think you have some interesting ideas, but that's all they are, ideas."

Sure of his ground he continues, "You've got no proof of what you're saying, and what's more you admit this guy could be dangerous. Even worse, you can't prove he *won't* kill anyone."

He then gives me his elusive, meaningless smile. "Why can't you be more specific about this guy? You counselors are all alike."

"Well, in a way you're right, Lieutenant," I answer. "I can't prove anything I've said, but I *do* think I *have* been specific about the way Dunn operates."

The Lieutenant then quickly grasps at a Custody decision about Dunn.

"Well, I think we ought to keep him here," he says. "Then if he doesn't get involved in the program to our satisfaction, we ought to send him to a maximum custody institution where he can really do some time the hard way."

What Chuvalo doesn't understand is that a maximum custody prison is really an easy place for a guy like Dunn to do time. The cons don't bother the staff, and the staff doesn't bother the cons. Both systems, in their ways, protect each other.

"What do the rest of you gentlemen think about Charlie's diagnosis and prognosis?" Palow asks.

There is no immediate response, until again Chuvalo speaks. "You're the doctor; you're supposed to have the answers to these so-called 'tough' cases."

Louis then apparently tries to appease the lieutenant.

"I think you do have a point, Lieutenant," he says, "about Dunn's not getting sufficiently involved in the program. I feel we can wait just so long for a man to make an effort toward change. Then if nothing happens, maybe we could think of other alternatives."

I knew it! That last statement has 'shock' written all over it. Chuvalo does not even attempt to hide his elation as he smiles at me. He has won another victory.

Suddenly I am getting angry again. For one thing, I think Louis is trying to play both sides. But for another, these quick decisions, without investigating every possible alternative before resorting to something like shock therapy frustrate the hell out of me.

But this is getting us nowhere. It is leading toward more danger for Dunn than he is to himself.

"Let's call in Dunn," I say, "and see what happens."

Everyone seems relieved when I make the suggestion.

Chuvalo presses the buzzer on the table which will bring Dunn into the room.

Dunn opens the door, walks in smiling at everyone, with even a special smile for Chuvalo. Maybe Dunn's charm will help swing the tide in his favor. He takes the empty chair at the far end of the table and seems anxious to get started.

I opened the interview with, "Why is it we're seeing you at the Classification Committee today?"

He looks rather puzzled. "Don't you remember?" he says. "I asked you for a job change and you said you'd bring me before the Committee."

"What are you doing now, *Mr.* Dunn?" Chuvalo asks him.

Jimmy responds quickly, "I've been in vocational welding for the past nineteen months."

Ed Small takes it up. He smiles at Dunn. "Isn't your name Jimmy?" He goes on, "Why do you want a job change? Have you finished the course?"

Dunn does not make any excuses, for which I am grateful.

"No," he responds, "but I want to be a hall porter."

That statement seems to set the whole committee off.
Thompson sounds like the usual schoolman. "What's a
porter's job prepare you for?" he asks. "You won't have a
trade; you don't have a high school diploma; in fact, the
way you are now, you're completely unskilled."

"That's not true," Dunn shoots back. "I have a trade,
I'm a bartender."

The committee simply sits and watches Dunn for a
minute, as though disbelieving him. Maybe he was a damn
good bartender and didn't need another trade. But there is
nothing that members of the staff like better than to put in
a man's file glowing reports of how much the inmate had
benefitted from a specific part of their program. The
academic people are ecstatic if an inmate completes the
high school program and finally receives his diploma, and
the vocational people are particularly gratified if an inmate
completes the year or two-year course. The fact that some
of the trades being taught are technologically outmoded, or
that there is little demand for some skills, or that in some
instances the training is too rudimentary to enable him to
get a job at the trade has apparently little to do with it.

Sansome, the vocational supervisor, seems hurt by
Dunn's response. "Now wait a minute, Dunn. Part of what
we're trying to do here is to give a man a skill so he'll be
better prepared when he leaves. What does a porter's job
prepare you for?"

I can't help but wonder what Dunn is thinking. He is
probably laughing up his blue-denim, well-starched sleeve. A
man is released from prison with about $20.00 or $30.00,
some new (but cheap) clothes, and little else. There he
goes, walking through the front gate, the well-dressed
parolee, looking like the country cousin in his Sunday best,
and his personals all neatly wrapped in a manila paper-
covered box. Usually, of course, the parolee has a job to go

to. But he has no transportation, because—even if he had money to buy a car—his driver's license has been revoked. If he's an addict, it's even worse—being society's latest scapegoat, it may take him as long as a year to get a license. So he has $20.00 and two weeks to go before he can get a paycheck. Usually he's just left all his friends in prison, and he has no one from whom to seek help. He is relegated to a cheap, fourth-class hotel with cracked ceilings, a small dirty sink, cobwebbed windows and brown curtains, the sickly smell of cooked cabbage, and friendly cockroaches. For company he has the best: drunks, pimps, whores, the feeble-minded, the incapacitated, vocational "rehabs," the poor, the lonely, the desperate. And, of course, he has a few of his own kind—parolees who are in the same grim boat.

Dunn is getting hostile. This is obvious in the tense position of his body, and his next responses make it plain to everyone.

"That doesn't have much to do with it," he answers. "I'm going to be here for a long time."

I know Chuvalo won't be able to resist that. Dunn couldn't resist saying it and Chuvalo can't help but react.

Chuvalo asks him sharply, "Then why do you want a porter's job? So you can wheel and deal?"

It is going badly. If Dunn gets too hostile, he will upset Palow and Custody and he will probably get shocked, or get shipped out to a maximum security prison. But if he is too passive and conforming, Chuvalo will say that Dunn is just doing time. If he sounds too healthy, *I* will become suspicious because I know that in group, Dunn is very secretive.

Dunn's response isn't too convincing.

"No, that's not it—look at my institutional record, I've never had a beef. Porters are needed, that's all, and I'd like the job."

A clean institutional record. That's what the staff likes to see. For the record, that means the man has never officially come to the attention of the Disciplinary Committee. But it means the inmate is really in a dilemma. On the one hand, the treatment staff asks to *see* the behavior, in the daily here-and-now situations, so the man can be worked with in an effort to change his behavior. On the other hand, if the inmate *does* become involved in a beef he is brought before the Committee. Hours are spent, first trying to figure out if the man is *really* guilty, then trying to find out why he became involved. I'll never forget the time an administrator spent two hours trying to find out "why" an inmate had two fresh eggs in his cell. As it turned out, someone else had rolled the eggs under his cell door, and the inmate had no knowledge of their being there. Another time an officer wrote a disciplinary report on an inmate he surprised while masturbating in his cell. One of the senior counselors saw the report before it got into the man's file and took it directly to his supervisor. The counselor wanted to have the report squelched on the grounds that masturbation is fairly common—both inside a prision and out of it. "Besides," he told his supervisor, "what about all of the staff members who masturbate in the privacy of their own homes when their wives refuse to have sex with them?" I loved that counselor after that.

"You don't sound too convincing to me," I say to Dunn. "I think you better go back to welding and complete the course; this would show some stability and maturity on your part."

Of course, I really don't believe that, but I feel I have to say it. My attempt to bring the meeting to an end only seems to upset Dunn.

"Wait a minute, here," he says. "Before you just shut this off—don't do this to me. Look at it from my angle. What am I doing in welding? You're the ones who are trying to make a welder out of me. The reason I got there in the first place was that it was the only thing open when I went to initial classification. I don't even *like* welding! I'll never do anything with it."

Sansome says, "I see by your grades in vocational welding that you haven't put out too much effort. You really haven't given it a chance. Maybe if you'd work at it a little you'd find you like it."

Dunn looks disgusted. "But look at it from my point again; how am I going to like something I just despise?"

I am beginning to become curious myself as to why he is pushing so hard for a job change. It couldn't only be the welding shop; he could do time, in any circumstances, standing on his head. I don't understand why he is being so insistent.

"Jimmy," I say, "what are you really trying to do with this porter's job, have a lot of free time?"

He doesn't answer my question, just gives out with a lot of words. "No, no," he responds, "I keep busy, I keep out of trouble, you can see that by my record."

I glance around the room, at the other members, but no one seems to want to pick it up.

"Well," I ask, "what do the rest of you gentlemen think?"

Small responds right away. I guess he can sense what I want to do.

"Since there seems to be some confusion about what to do with this man," he says, "we'll postpone a decision for four weeks and hold another classification meeting at that time."

Everyone seems relieved, but Dunn. He gets up quickly and leaves the room. The rest of us look around at one another with that polite, getting-ready-to-leave look. Perhaps each of us—in our different ways—is glad that another classification has ended.

Chapter 4

The
Story Hour

DUNN:

We had a little action yesterday. Charlie Durko, a known snitch—got on the witness stand and everything—got six inches of steel put into his kidney. Pete Ramirez, one of the guys Charlie snitched on in his extended career as a paid informer for the Narcotics Bureau, got him on the second tier. While four of his *compadres* formed a half-circle, Pete tried to end the snitch's career. The only trouble is, snitches are hard to kill! Charlie's lying up in the hospital getting along fine. The doctor's very optimistic, saying he'll be able to live a long life on one kidney.

The funny thing, however, is that Charlie wouldn't tell who hit him. I guess he does have a little pride after all. Or maybe he only snitches to the bulls on the street. Anyway, when Pete found out that Charlie would be all right, he just knew he had a one-way ticket to the Fortress. So far, according to the convict-orderlies in the hospital, Charlie has yet to tell them what happened or who did it. Lieutenant Chuvalo and Captain Thurlow have really been pressuring him, but the guy's holding up.

That means we're going to have a lot of action, too, in group today. The bulls know that there were forty guys in the unit at the time Charlie got his, which also means there's going to be big-time pressure in the group to get somebody to give up the executioner. Group will be a ball today! On most days it's simply a drag. You can't find out anything or get any kind of information. Hell, I've been trying to find out for over a year why at first they wouldn't give me a job change. And then, for some damn reason, they gave it to me without even having to go to classification!

I know there's going to be pressure, and the staff is going to be hitting at the weakest spots in the group trying to come up with the knifer. But I also know that nobody has the guts to give up somebody in front of 150 convicts. The only snitching that's done in the penitentiary is done on the sly, in the Custody Office, Lieutenant's office, or to one of the snitch's favorite bulls. But by far the strangest method of snitching is through the inmate Interview Request Box where the anonymous snitches write all their notes and drop them in, where they don't even get credit for their snitching! All of the staff's good little snitches will be just aching to come up with the guilty party. But they know they can't in group because steel will be waiting for them, too.

This'll be good. I know Murray is just waiting to get into that group so he can show what a good prison worker he is by getting the men to come up with the assailant. There is just a possibility he might do it because he's got some of these hoosiers around here so twisted they don't know whether they're coming or going.

The guys in the unit were all sloughed right after Charlie became a celebrity. We were let out this morning. There was nothing else but talk of Charlie's mishap. In the mess hall the whole joint was buzzing with the good news. Tommy and I cut it up at breakfast and could hardly wait to get in the group after chow to see the action.

Everyone came back to the unit from breakfast in an excited mood. Like always when we got back from breakfast the chairs were all arranged in rows, making a circle for 150 men on the cellblock floor. The guys took their seats quickly this morning because it was going to be a good group. They were laughing, scratching, and cutting-up touches. When Murray came in, the joint quieted down to a faint buzz. With Murray was Henderson, Murray's boss, who looked pretty worried this morning. In fact, he looked as if he was about to have a baby!

Tommy and I took our usual seats in the farthest row of the circle away from the bulls. Murray had seated himself in his usual position in the inner circle of the group. Henderson had taken a chair in the third row of the circle, directly opposite Murray.

Though I hate these goddamn groups, sometimes they're kind of interesting. In fact, you get a lot of laughs out of listening to these hoosiers cry. There's a saying: "There's nothing as sad as a grown man crying," but really it's not as sad as it is funny. These guys cry as though they were going to get something for their crying. The only thing they've got coming is a hard time on a rough road. But today ought to be the most interesting group we've had so far. I've been sitting in here every morning now since they started this group and already I've learned how many hundreds of ways there are for a grown man to cry.

After everyone has taken his seat and the joint quiets down from the customary noise before a group, it's almost as though everybody freezes. You can hear a pin drop. Henderson, who's seated almost directly in front of me, is bent over in his chair with his elbows on his knees. He looks pretty tense. Murray, across from him, is looking his usual blasé self with his arms folded across his chest and his knees crossed, sitting half sidesaddle in the chair and gazing out just over the tops of everybody's head. He tries to give the impression that he is seeing and thinking things nobody else can. But then, there is always the possibility that he is as clever as he thinks he is.

The silence mounts. Silence in a closed group of 150 men can get to be pretty oppressive in a short time. But it is an effective weapon. The one thing the staff can't cope with in group is silence. But I know this morning that if we give them the continual silence bit, because of what happened yesterday, things will really explode around here. I had had a little action yesterday myself—gotten into my first penitentiary beef. It was a hummer beef, but might be good enough to distract the tension. So after the silence keeps mounting, I finally have to say something to break it.

"I got a disciplinary report yesterday."

When I say that in the silent group, it is almost as though a great relief comes over the room. Men start moving and shifting around in their chairs; the tension has been broken.

Ryder, one of the guys I know pretty well, knows what I am doing and answers, "What did you get it for?"

"I had a poem in my locker when they shook it down."

Corici, one of Murray's *better men*, gives me some static.
I can see that I am finally going to have to straighten that
turd out. He's run his mouth once too often. I'll have to
jack him up after group and ask him what the fuck he
thinks he's talking to me like that for?

A bunch of the guys then start kicking the poem thing
around. Things are really going good. The group is shifting
around and enjoying this little bit we have going. We all
know what the staff want us to be talking about. I take a
quick look at both Murray and Henderson to see if they
are enjoying the joke. Murray still has his Buddha-like look
on his face, and Henderson is still in his crouched position.

The lame, Corici, starts needling me again. I start not to
answer the turd but know that if I don't it will give the
staff an in to ask my reasons.

Corici is really worrying it. That makes it definite; I am
going to have to straighten him out. Maybe a few lumps on
his head will give him the idea.

Thurlinger, who is trying to get a parole, comes up with
some support for Corici. I guess I will have to straighten
him out, too. That fat-faced asshole makes me hot every
time he opens his mouth in the group. Every convict wants
to get out of the penitentiary, but thank God, very few of
them will go as far as he will to do it.

"I think it's a nothing beef and they're just fuckin' with
me again," I say.

Murray finally comes out of his trance. "We're getting
into a hopeless argument here. I think there are several
things happening here this morning. First of all, I think
you're talking about this to avoid talking about what
happened yesterday. Secondly, we're not going to resolve
anything in this group about Dunn's involvement with this
poem thing because he hasn't been to disciplinary yet.
Furthermore, this group can't decide for the Custody staff

whether *This Is My Beloved* is pornographic or not. I've read it myself and I don't think so—but even that's beside the point."

The whole group has been waiting for Murray to come on with one of those famous two-edged remarks. He's always doing that, saying one thing and meaning five others. But nobody has anything to say. In fact, the group gets very quiet again. They also know that he only uses those opening gambits to get somebody to respond so he can begin messing with their melons.

The tension starts to mount again. The silence goes on two, three, four, five minutes. I know better than to say anything this time.

Finally, after six or seven minutes, Jimenez says, "Hey, 'Chuco,' aren't you going home next week?"

"Yeah, I'm finally getting outa here."

Price, who must not be thinking too good this morning, says, "You're lucky, man. This is no place to be, especially now!"

The goddamn fool. Doesn't he realize he's playing right into Murray's hands? The first time somebody starts talking about, or even makes a reference to Charlie's getting his yesterday, we're in for a real jackpot.

But Tabouri, a good convict, comes up quickly with, "Yeah, you won't have to eat this fucking slop anymore, or listen to this bullshit."

That seems to make up for Price's slip; however, it also sends Henderson off into one of his famous rages.

"What's going on in this goddamn group?"

Silence.

Henderson again. "Don't you know what happened here yesterday? Are you ignorant of it? A man was hurt!"

Then the laugh of the day comes. Tommy seated next to me, and a few rows behind Henderson, says, in a low tone

but just loud enough for most of the group to hear, "Fuck
that snitch."

There are a few quick laughs, but they are cut off fast
when Henderson wheels around in his seat and with his
face getting that well-known, blood-red look, shouts, "Who
said that?"

He looks hard at all of us seated behind him, each one in
turn, and as he looks, he gets more and more red.

"You bunch of bastards!" He wheels back around toward the rest of the group. "You're just trying to protect
each other. Half of this group was there, saw the knifing,
and you're all trying to protect the guilty party. You're all
guilty! Even you, Gonzales. You're going home next week
and what are you doing to help us with this problem? The
Parole Board felt you were ready to go home; what did
they do, make a mistake?"

He keeps looking around the group. He is working himself into a fit. All I can think of to myself is, "That dirty,
red-necked, Irish son-of-a-bitch! Because he's a bull and
we're convicts, he thinks he can talk to us like we're a
piece of shit."

When no one responds he goes on shouting, and all he
gets for his pains, besides high blood pressure, is complete
hostility from all of us.

Another prolonged silence greets his last outburst.

Finally Murray says, "Well, I guess it is difficult to get
people to change. Here I've been thinking we've been
coming along pretty good in this group. We've made some
decisions which have helped make this a smoother running
unit."

He pauses, looks around the group for a weak spot he
can put to his own use.

"But here now," he goes on, "apparently we can't meet
our first real challenge. Some of the men here I thought
had been coming along real well."

Again he looks around the group, seeking support. He catches Johnson's eye and looks steadily at him for a minute. Then he puts big-time pressure on him. He really puts Johnson on the spot. Johnson's a three-time loser and has a reputation for being a good convict. But Murray comes on to him with something about the "talk in the office" business they'd had which sets up an expression, and makes everyone wonder just what they were *talking about* "in the office."

Johnson knows he is on the spot. "I wish I could, but I don't know anything about it."

"What do you mean you don't know anything about it," Murray answers. "You were here in the unit when it happened."

"Yeah, that's right, but I still didn't see anything. It's a big unit."

Johnson has to do that, he has no choice. Even if he is trying to get his time set on his third straight second-degree burglary, he can't go any other route. He knows he's going to do a bundle of time because he's got himself pegged as a repeater.

Of course, there's the possibility that Murray might try and help Johnson get his time set, which might tempt him. But he doesn't have any guarantee what Murray, or any of the rest of these sons-of-bitches are going to do. In the meantime, he's still got to live here with us. So, he's too smart to gamble on a shaky winner on the come when he knows he's got a sure thing now. Maybe being outside would be better, but at least here he knows what he has to face. To go along with them doesn't give him anything he can count on.

Murray knows right away he's lost with Johnson, but he isn't through with the rest of us. "Well, isn't there anyone here who wants to help himself enough to help us?" he says. "After all, you guys are the ones that need the help."

Another silence greets his challenge.

Now, I guess he's trying to shame some of us by coming on with a lot of crap about all he is doing for us and how little we are doing in turn. But he ruins it by saying something about helping him to help us.

Help him to help us! God! Every day he comes up with the same lame-ass bullshit as though he expects somebody to believe him.

"I thought we would have a real therapeutic unit here," he goes on with his pitch, still pushing, still looking around the group. "But I guess not. It makes me wonder what I'm doing here."

Silence.

Murray knows he is beat for the day. "Well, we didn't accomplish much this morning. We'll meet again tomorrow. Group's over."

When we all file out on our way to work, the staff pulls into a group about the group. What the hell is left for them to say? It's obvious we've won another round, just like we'll keep on winning.

The
Group Meeting

MURRAY:

As I entered the front gate in the morning, the tower officer called down to me, "That you, Murray?"

"Who'd you expect at this hour, Jesus Christ?" It was only 7:15 A.M., at least forty-five minutes before the bulk of the day shift would arrive, and nothing usually happens at night.

He leaned out of his tower, cupping his hands around his mouth and shouted, "There's been a knifing in your unit."

A knifing! Jesus Christ! Why? I wondered who did it. I thought the group members were under better control. I wasn't as much concerned about the victim as I was about the person who still saw that kind of behavior as a way of settling differences.

But what was of even more importance to me was how the group would respond to the incident. It was in these kinds of situations, when the issues were clear, that we expected the group to become productive. It was around these kinds of things that a real dividing line became apparent, and it was here where the internal systems were most openly in conflict. Custody wanted the assailant. Treatment wanted to use the issue as a way to examine behavior. The inmates closed off, shut down all communication in an effort to protect themselves.

The victim and the assailant became secondary issues. It was just like the Gideon or the Escobebo cases, when really they as individuals were soon forgotten. But it was the ripples created by their precedents which continue to influence penal institutions. If the group could bring some kind of order out of the chaos created by this specific situation and galvanize their efforts to bring about an examination of behavior, then, the real purpose of the group—which is to help men in prison change their values—could be realized.

The tower officer went on, "Now let's see how effective your group work is. See if you can get these slobs to tell what son-of-a-bitch shanked that snitch."

"O.K., Mr. Burns," I responded as indirectly as I could. "Maybe you're right about group work. Maybe it creates more problems than it solves."

He almost gloated in response as he opened the electrically controlled gate, and I went through.

The atmosphere inside the main corridor wasn't particularly unusual this morning. Some of the men waiting in the mess hall lines were a little more animated, but that could mean anything. Some of them waved to me as I walked by toward my unit, others said hello with their eyes, while a few ignored my greeting and looked away. I tried to appear as calm as I possibly could; I didn't want to touch off any more anxiety than was already there.

When I walked into the unit, some of the first-watch officers, who would be going off shortly, nodded to me. They silently appeared to be carrying the weight of the world on their shoulders. It didn't happen on their watch; I don't know why they should have been worried. It had happened shortly after the third watch came on, but perhaps, like a chain reaction, they thought they had been derelict in their duties in the recent past and had somehow precipitated the attack.

I was kind of upset by it, but only because it had happened in my unit. Prison workers have a way of becoming intensely personal about their units. They'll tell you they know all of the men in their unit by their first names, but are relatively unconcerned about men in other units. I had grown used to killings and knifings in prison. It was one of the expectations of the job. I know one thing— whenever we did have a stabbing or a killing, or something else of major importance, it seemed to create a great deal of excitement among the staff and inmates. Almost as if these incidents were needed to inject some life into a colorless existence.

Slowly the men began to wander into the unit. Maybe it was my own anxiety, but I felt there was a distinct reluctance on their part to meet this morning. Of course, there are always the men who resist the idea *every* morning. "Group gunselling" they call it. "Gunselling" is a prison term which refers to the behavior of the younger men in prison, a kind of horseplay without any serious meaning, a kind of attention-getting device.

The chairs were in place. This was good. It would give us a start. Sometimes, when the men really resisted, they would "forget" to put the chairs in the circle, and this would waste at least five minutes of the group time.

A few stragglers were late as usual. A couple of staff members, vocational people, were also late, having their morning coffee, I supposed, in the staff canteen, talking about their next proposed five-percent raises.

*   *   *

Now we can start. I can feel more tension than usual. There is complete silence. It goes on, one minute, two minutes, five minutes. It is becoming unbearable. I wonder who can stand it least, the staff or the men.

While the silence keeps mounting, I try to pull together my thoughts on how best to get the group in a position where they will: (1) deal with the incident; (2) *really* talk about it and what it means; and (3) ideally, come forward with the assailant.

I know it will be a tough job because of the fierce allegiance most of the men have to the inmate code, but I am determined that this is a good issue to focus on and might be the spark to bring some change in this group.

It turns out the men can stand the tension least. Dunn finally breaks the silence.

"I got a disciplinary report yesterday," he says.

Oh my God! How can he do this? After all the individual time I've spent on that man I can, at the very least, expect some cooperation, but not for him to try to completely undermine the group. I don't necessarily expect him to talk about the knifing, but neither do I expect him to totally deny it by ignoring it. I feel he does owe me something, too. After all, when he was in trouble after that bad classification meeting last year, I eventually got it straightened out so he could remain here.

Inmate Ryder responds to him. Ryder is an old-timer—murder first—who stomped his wife to death when she accused him of being impotent and flaunted her lovers in his face. The rage inside of him is now quite calm, but he will do at least twelve to fourteen years before he will get out again.

"What did you get it for?" he asks.

That is no help. I stare at Dunn, hoping to attract his attention so that he will respond as he knows he should. But he will not look my way.

"I had a poem in my locker when they shook it down," he answers.

The "shakedown," is a device used by Custody to tell the inmates in a rather blunt and direct manner that they're not trusted. And they're not.

Inmate Corici says to Dunn, "A poem! Are you trying to kid the group? You don't get disciplinaries for having poems."

Corici could really be a lot of help in group if he wanted to. He's one of those rare individuals, the true first offender in prison: twenty-five years old, in for a series of burglaries. Ran up against a tough, politically ambitious prosecutor and an unsympathetic judge, so he didn't get probation. A good solid probation officer would have been equally effective; instead it's costing the State three thousand dollars a year to keep him. Corici's caught in a dilemma. The inmates don't listen to him because they don't trust him; moreover, he doesn't take a strong enough stand to please the staff. So what it amounts to is that he's going to be infected with the inmate culture and the staff isn't going to be able to use him effectively.

"It was probably a fuck book."

That comment brings general laughter. Even the staff has
to laugh. Inmate Estrada said it. Estrada, twenty-three-
year-old Mexican-American, ex-marine. He, along with two
others, had jumped a couple in lovers' lane, dragged the girl
off and forced her to copulate with each of them. She
wound up in a mental hospital. The case was something
like Chessman's, except these guys would do only three to
five years. She was a ghetto girl, and there was no publicity.

Estrada in many ways is fairly representative of the
Mexican-American inmate we get in our institutions.
Usually they speak a corrupt Mexican slang, have barely
managed to finish elementary school, are unskilled in any
trade, and most important, are not really motivated toward
doing anything about themselves.

Dunn quiets the group by responding, "No, no, man, it
was a fuckin' poem, Walter Benton's *This is My Beloved.*
Captain Thurlow says its's pornographic."

Goddamn it! How can we expect to make any headway
in this business when we have staff like Thurlow? He
literally got into the business by the kitchen door. He
started as a cook. He's been in the system twenty years.
His real name is Anastasious Thaslanios; he changed it to
Thurlow. The inmates found out about his Greek background and nicknamed him "The Greasy Greek." In time,
Thurlow went from the kitchen to Custody because the
chances for promotion there were better. He took a few
extension courses at college, and this qualified him for the
"professional development" section that is found in every
Civil Service application form. He thinks he's on his way to
becoming warden and then he can really do things his own
way.

Thomas speaks up, "I read that last time I was out.
What's pornographic about it?"

I guess that's all Thomas read, too. He was only out forty-eight hours! A good example of how little prison touches some of these guys. Thomas is a two-time loser, alcoholic check-writer. Every time he comes back he joins Alcoholics Anonymous immediately. A.A. is another organization which needs deviants to survive. It's like prison—if there were only a few alcoholics, there would be no A.A., and if there were only a few convicts, no prisons. Thomas was doomed to come back again and again until he was old enough to become a fixture at the state's approximation of Sun City. There it is, the *Old Man's Colony*, where all they do is bask in the sun, relax, and read all day, watch television, play checkers, and barely realize that Custody is around. The department has provided a home for its retired lawbreakers.

Dunn continues the farce, "It's just a love-poem. I don't know why it's pornographic. You tell me why."

Corici adds to my frustration. "When are you going to the Disciplinary Committee?"

I am really very anxious at this point. I don't know how much more I can take, before I have to intervene.

Corici and Dunn pursue the topic as though it has tremendous importance. Here is a clear case where the inmates are bent on not talking about the important issue, but instead spending time on lesser items to protect themselves.

Dunn answers Corici's question. "Tomorrow."

The group allows Corici and Dunn to continue their question and answer session.

"What do you think is going to happen?" Corici asks.

"Hell, I don't know. I didn't even know the fuckin' thing was against the rules."

At this point inmate Thurlinger gets into the act. Now I know we're dead, or at least will be held up even longer.

Thurlinger has a way of intellectualizing everything, beating it to death, so that little of any real value remains. He is a bright, articulate, and bitter man who tends to look down on the other inmates and almost all of the staff. An embezzler, he took hundreds of thousands from his employer. He thought they would not prosecute because of the bad publicity, but they fooled him.

"That doesn't make any difference," Thurlinger says. "Ignorance of the law is no excuse."

"Who in the fuck asked you?" Dunn answers. "I think it's a nothin' beef. They're just fuckin' with me again. It's just like they wouldn't give me that job change a year ago."

I've had it! I will have to intervene to try to switch the group. I know what is happening, and I'm sure everyone else does. I seem to be getting no support from staff, not even my boss, Henderson, who can at least be depended upon for some moralizing once in a while. As administrator of the unit, he should be much more active. Maybe he is waiting to see what I want to do with the group, or maybe he is just plain scared.

"We're getting into a hopeless argument here," I say. "I think there are several things that are happening this morning. First of all, I think you're talking about this to avoid talking about what happened yesterday. Secondly, we're not going to resolve anything here about Dunn's involvement with this poem thing because he hasn't been to disciplinary yet. Furthermore, this group can't decide for the Custody staff whether *This Is My Beloved* is pornographic or not. I've read it myself, and I don't think so, but even that's beside the point."

For months now, I have been working with this group, every day for an hour, in an attempt to get them to start talking about themselves. For a time, it looked as if we were making some progress. We have handled some important problems in the group, such as the men stealing from each other; one or two of the men had talked about the loneliness they felt in prison; others talked about their confused sexual feelings in an all-male environment.

Obviously, I have been too optimistic. My remarks are greeted with silence—another five minutes of deadly silence. The tension starts mounting again.

Finally inmate Jimenez breaks the silence.

"Hey, 'Chuco'," he says, "aren't you going home next week?"

"Yeah," Gonzales responds, "I'm finally gettin' outa here."

After weeks of being overdue on his parole date because he could not find suitable employment, a distant uncle came through with some sort of a job offer at $1.50 per hour. I wondered whether it was a genuine offer or just another bogus job to meet the parole requirements so he could get out.

Help comes from an unexpected corner. I'm sure it is an accident, but inmate Price says, "You're lucky, man, this is no place to be, especially now."

I grab at it immediately. "What do you mean, Price?"

But before he can answer, inmate Tabouri, who pretends he didn't hear my question, says, "Yeah, you won't have to eat this fuckin' slop anymore or listen to this bullshit."

As suddenly as the opening showed itself, it closes over again.

At this point I have pretty well decided to let the group take its own course. I hope that eventually some of the stronger members of the group will take it upon themselves to tackle the problem.

"What's going on in this goddamn group!"

Like an electrifying charge, Jack Henderson's voice cuts
into the group. The program administrator's shrill tone
catches the group in the midst of their play-acting. Everything comes to an immediate stop.

Jack is a career man in the true sense of the word, one
of the many workers in the department with a Master of
Social Work degree. The social work school stresses meeting
the individual's "needs," but in a prison setting this concept is unworkable. All it does is reinforce the basic pathology and give the individual a further excuse for his
behavior. He means well, but he can become so angry when
the men do not meet his expectations that he will almost
lose control. It is as if he expects total cooperation from
the inmates; for them to be "nice guys" and not cause any
trouble. He tries hard at his job as administrator of treatment programs, but he knows very little about treatment
and less about inmates. The men, derisively, call him
"Granny" Henderson. They have a saying: "Granny
Henderson lived in a shoe. She had so many children, she
didn't know what to do." On at least one occasion, he
heard an inmate recite the ditty. He didn't laugh at it,
which would have been the easiest way to handle it, but
neither did it make him angry. He attributed it to the
inmates' hostility and lack of maturity, totally ignored it,
and not for a moment did he consider how it might apply
to him.

I am afraid that if he gets out of control in this situation
it will only serve to further antagonize the men and drive
the wedge between staff and inmate even further. Everyone
is silent, but it is the kind of silence that simply shouts
hostility.

"Don't you know what happened here yesterday?" he
goes on. "Are you ignorant of it? A man was hurt!"

There is no stopping him now. He is so angry he can barely talk coherently. His body is visibly shaking.

An unidentified voice from across the room, almost in an aside, says, "Fuck that snitch!"

Jack screams, as he wheels around in his seat. "Who said that?" He jerks off his glasses, as though preparing to fight, his face flushing a scarlet red.

"You bunch of bastards," he goes on. "No one cares that a man was hurt. You're just trying to protect each other. Half of this group was there, saw the knifing and you're all lying to protect the guilty party. You're all guilty! Even you, Gonzales. You're going home next week, and what are you doing to help us with this problem?"

Yeah, what is Gonzales doing but protecting his parole date and his reputation as a good, solid, nonsnitching convict? After all, if he knows anything about the knifing and does mention it in group, there will naturally be an investigation, evidence will be given in a court of law, the man who did the knifing will most likely be found guilty and be given more time. Here we are asking a group to deal with a problem, with almost definite assurance that retribution will be the result.

Henderson continues to side-track the group with his harangue at Gonzales.

"The Board felt you were ready to go home; what did they do, make a mistake?"

The group remains silent. I find it difficult to give Henderson any real support as long as he is so angry. I am casting about in my mind for a way to turn the group, but at the same time to stay on the subject.

"This is an old group," Jack continues. "And you bastards are acting like a new one!"

He won't let go. "Here we are trying to help you, and you won't give us anything! You're not interested in us or your families. You're not even interested in yourselves. All care about is that goddamn code!"

More silence greets him.

It is getting close to the end of the hour. I am disappointed in the way they have handled the whole thing. Not that I ever expected them to turn up the guilty party, but I guess I did expect them to discuss the incident, rather than pretend it never happened.

"Well," I say, "as I hear what is happening this morning, the staff is saying one thing, the men are saying something quite different. It is difficult to get people to change. Here I've been thinking we've been coming along pretty good in this group. We've made some decisions which have helped make this a smoother-running unit; we've also had a chance to discuss some real personal problems. But now, apparently, we can't meet our first real challenge."

As I say this I glance around the entire group, trying to take in all of the men.

"Some of the men here," I continue, "I thought had been coming along real well. You, for instance, Johnson. We've talked about some of these things in the office. I thought we were developing a real tight relationship. What do you think? Can't you help us with this problem?"

This is going to be my last desperate move, and it is a decided gamble. I don't really know how strong Johnson is or can be in this instance. Eddie Johnson—a study in contrasts, but above all, an unknown commodity. When he first came to the institution, he was practically hallucinating. It was not picked up right away because he was so quiet. A few individual sessions in my office revealed how disturbed he really was. But, rather than ship him off to the medical facility, I let him know how disturbed I thought he was and at the same time gave him a lot of support. He could help me here, and I am hoping he feels indebted. He is very perceptive and is a fast thinker, but at the same time, a real cautious con man.

"I wish I could, but I don't know anything about it," he responds, trying to maintain his composure. He knows he is on trial in front of his peers, and if he gives the slightest inch, he will have to undergo one hell of a lot of pressure.

"What do you mean, you don't know anything about it? You were here in the unit when it happened." I feel I will have to continue to pressure him.

Johnson looks at me, obviously harrassed, perhaps because he has an inkling of what I am thinking.

"Yeah, that's right," he responds, "but I still didn't see anything. It's a big unit."

I give up on Johnson. I slowly look around the room, weighing each person's strength. The thought keeps going through my mind: "Isn't there at least one person here who can help?"

I verbalize the thought. "Well—isn't there anyone here who wants to help himself enough to help us? After all, you guys are the ones that need the help."

I feel myself getting angry, or perhaps merely disgusted.

"You mean I've been working with this group," I say, "meeting every day, five days a week, and this is all I can expect? With some of the guys I thought I had a real relationship. And I thought you could help me to help you! I thought we could have a real therapeutic unit here. But I guess not. It makes me wonder what I'm doing here."

And I do wonder what I am doing here. The whole thing does have an air of hopelessness about it.

More silence greets the comments. I receive a few unsympathetic looks from the two vocational teachers in the group. Henderson is still obviously having trouble controlling himself.

"Well," I finally say, with a degree of resignation, "we didn't accomplish too much here this morning. We'll meet again tomorrow. Group's over."

The men rise, rather subdued I think, and file out—on their way to their respective trades or classrooms. The staff members gather their chairs into a smaller group in preparation for the postsession.

"How did you think it went, Jack?" I ask Henderson. I think I will give him a chance, first, to ventilate some of his feelings.

"I got so gosh-darned mad in there," he answers. "I saw the men as being completely ungrateful."

He looks rather sheepish regarding his leadership, which he apparently sees now as a failure. But, nevertheless, he is able to be fairly honest about his feelings.

Mr. Fowler, one of the vocational teachers, seems nervous, but is also able to be fairly honest.

"I don't blame you for being angry," he says to Henderson, "now you see why we're not sold on these groups. I really feel that a more well-rounded program for the men is needed."

"We're not here to evaluate the program," I say sharply, "but to evaluate the group."

Mr. Phillips, the other vocational teacher, says, "You're being a little touchy, Mr. Murray."

At that I almost feel like laughing at myself.

"Yes," I answer, "I guess I am rather on edge, but no staff member likes a stabbing in his unit. I do feel that you guys could have been more helpful."

"I don't know what we could have done," Fowler says. "Actually, I think you're being unrealistic. These guys aren't going to give you what you're asking for."

"I don't think we're asking for too much," Jack says. "All we're asking is that they help each other."

"I'm not sure I agree with you, Jack," I say. "We're asking a lot of the men. We're asking that they break the code, that they truly start caring for each other. In a large measure, in a prison, it's every man for himself, and this is even true on the outside. For example, look at the Genovese killing."

I remind him of the New York killing where over thirty people had heard a woman's cries for help and not one helped her or even phoned the police.

"What makes us think," I go on, "that guys in here are going to be any different? After all, they were once a part of society and that's where they learned their values."

Henderson looks at his watch, and seems uncomfortable.

"Enough of this philosophizing," he says, "it's too early in the morning and I've got to get to work."

He rises, nods to me, and leaves the unit. The teachers follow, and suddenly I am left alone.

Chapter 5

The
Good Time

DUNN:

I always get to the gym first. That's one of the reasons I hassled so much to get the porter's job, so I can get to the gym before the rest of the weight-lifters. This way I'm sure to get the weights and equipment I need.

Working out is good; I'm always the healthiest guy in the penitentiary. It's great to have seventeen-inch arms! You walk down the corridor, knowing you're big, and knowing that no one else wants to mess with you. I see how the other guys look at me because of my size. It's a look of envy and fear, and I use it for all it's worth.

Because I always get to the gym first, I have the weights and equipment saved for my work-out partners by the time they get there, directly after lunch. I always have to sit and wait and hold the equipment until Buddy Johnson and Huey Parsons get there.

Buddy is big and strong, but in a barrel-like way. Most of his strength is in his shoulders and arms with a lot of driving power from his back. His best lifts are overhead lifts: militaries and behind-the-necks. Huey is just the opposite, tall and lanky, with smooth, rippling muscles that look bigger than they are simply because of his tallness and the smallness of his bone structure.

As penitentiaries go, this is a reasonably new one, and the gym and equipment are still in pretty good shape. The gym is huge, bigger than regulation size, and it doubles as an auditorium with a stage at one end, directly opposite the entrance doors. For the minimal entertainment they have here—mostly movies—they set up chairs on the gym floor. The biggest problem with the gym doubling as a theater is that when they're showing movies and have shut the doors, the place gets warm, and the smell of sweat is almost overpowering.

The gym floor gleams with the daily work and attention that is given to it by the inmates who are assigned to the gym crew. The walls are clean and painted a pastel color. I know they believe that if they can contain us and keep us reasonably happy with playthings and toys and pretty colors we won't be any problem for them. But I use the gym because I enjoy it. I like to work out, and I like to be big. But I also know that it's a fight between me and what I use the gym for, and between them and why they have it here for my use. I hate to go along with their game and play into their hands, but I enjoy working out too much to quit.

The gym is divided into three sections. The section closest to the door is half of the gym, where a full-length basketball court is almost constantly in use. Half of the remainder, on the right-hand side, is used by the boxers, wrestlers, and tumblers, and is equipped with ring mats and all of the paraphernalia those people use. The remaining quarter of the gym is reserved for the weight-lifters. This, too, has mats on the floor to protect the hardwood finish from the crash of the weights and is equipped with benches, incline-boards, weights, bars, and dumbbells. They are racked up on stands over on the wall when not in use.

As soon as I get into the gym, I head straight for the weight pile, get the bar, the four hundred pounds of weight we'll need, the dumbbells, incline bench, and a bench and lay them out in the area where we'll work. Then I just sit there on the bench, to hold the equipment, and wait until Buddy and Huey get there. The gym slowly starts to fill up with guys coming from the messhall. Some guys come to work out, some to train in the ring, and other guys change and get the constant basketball game going.

Buddy comes in first. He works in the bakery and gets out while the mess line is still running. It's a good place for a weight-lifter to work because he can eat all he wants. Buddy gets off work before Huey comes out of the mess-hall with the rest of his unit.

"Good old dependable Jimmy," Buddy says as he walks across the floor toward me. "You're always here and got the stuff."

"Naturally. That's the way its supposed to be."

"Where's Huey?" Buddy asks. "He should be here by now. What's the matter; is he dragging his feet again? You know how he is. Sometimes you got to drag him here to work out. He's always saying he's sick or something. He's got more illnesses than any weight-lifter I ever saw."

"Oh, Huey'll be here. I saw him a little while ago. Did you bring any goodies from the bakery?"

"No, that shit-heel, Sergeant Cummings, is running the kitchen today. He shakes down too good. I don't do anything when he's on."

Buddy keeps his work-out partners supplied with goodies and other foods that weight-lifters need. Prison diets aren't exactly high-protein. His best concoction is an instant cocoa which he makes in the bakery using state supplies. He takes cocoa, powered milk, sugar, a little nutmeg, some other ingredients that I don't know about, and mixes them and sifts them together in a formula he developed himself. He ought to patent it when he gets out. He smuggles it out of the bakery and past the shakedown strapped to his legs. It makes a good quick-energy drink after a workout. All you have to do is add hot water, and there you have it, instant strength. He also supplies us with honey he gets out of the bakery in plastic flasks strapped to his leg. We always eat three spoons of honey just before a workout and three spoons of honey just after. Honey is great for the hard work you have to do; it's a natural food and also gives great reservoirs of immediately converted energy.

While Buddy and I wait for Huey, we watch a couple of middleweights who have changed into sweatsuits and trunks and are working out in the ring. One of them is Windy Wilkins, a guy everyone says would have been middleweight champion if he could have stayed out of the joint. But he's got a story like a lot of these people around these shit-houses: a lot of talent but can't keep himself out of the penitentiary. They were going good, sparring around—not heavy, they didn't have headgear on—but fast work, with the emphasis on defense. The other guy is another of Windy's protegés whom he's turning out in his words to be "a champ, man." He's always training somebody to be champ. If he can't make it, maybe one of his boys will.

Huey finally arrives on the scene with that deceptively slow walk, which, because of his long legs actually has him covering distances quickly.

"Come on, man, you're holding up the show."

"I got hung up, Buddy," Huey answers. "But now your daddy Huey is here and everything is all right."

"Yeah, you're my daddy," Buddy shoots back, "but I fuck all my daddies."

"Well, maybe you can fuck me sometime," Huey says. "We'll talk about it later."

"Come on you guys, quit fucking around," I say, "let's get this workout on; I got muscles to build."

We set the bench up for bench presses and load on 225 pounds, our warm-up weight. Huey gets down first on the bench—flat, arching his back with his arms extended over his head—ready for Buddy and me to hand him the weight. We hand the weight up from the floor to him and he shakes it a few times to get the feel of it, and then begins doing his bench presses. He slowly lets the weight down till it touches his massive chest and then back up to arms extended. This he does ten times to get warm. Buddy gets down next, and I follow him to repeat the same procedure.

Then we start adding weight. We each do six with 250, four with 275, and three with three hundred pounds. We have a regular routine. First we do bench presses, then pullovers, military presses, behind the neck presses, dumb-bell chest work, french curls, tricep extensions, and regular curls.

We work every day. On alternate days we do upper-body work; on the other days we do lower extremities work. Squats for the legs, and stomach work for the rippling stomach effect. We're really in good shape!

It's funny; on the streets I do everything in the world to tear myself down physically. But in the joint I'm the healthiest guy around. Sometimes it doesn't make sense even to me.

Our whole jolt in this penitentiary revolves around working out and getting bigger and stronger. The workout is the high point of my day. It's what we look forward to each day and what we contemplate at night. Moreover, we're constantly talking about what three-month routine we'll go on next.

We like two of the exercises in our present routine better than the rest. I guess it's because we get a lot of laughs and kidding from the other guys who are around working out. When we do pullovers, we use so much weight—up to four hundred pounds—one guy has to hold you down. It's done by lying flat on the bench with your head over the end, while the weight rests on your chest. From there you bring the weight up off your chest, over your face, and down, and touch the floor, and then back. With that much weight on one end of the bench, it would automatically flip you, and you'd go over on your head if somebody didn't sit on your legs and hold you down. We take turns sitting on each other's legs, holding the person doing the pullovers by the belt so he doesn't tip over backwards. The strain is tremendous, and once Huey's belt broke and he lost his pants, besides almost going over on his head.

The other exercise we like is tricep extensions. In order to do those, you have to have two benches, placed about four feet apart. You put your hands on one and your feet on the other and stretch yourself out between them. Then we sit on each other's lap while the guy doing the exercise, by the strength of his arms, lowers himself down and then back up ten times. With a two hundred pound man sitting on his middle, it makes quite an exercise. It's great for the triceps, the backs of the arms. The backs of my arms are huge and look great.

While we're working out we kibitz and cut-up touches and have a hell of a time. Like I said, the workout is the high point of my day, and I really look forward to it. They can keep their groups, their school, and the trades. I want nothing to do with them. The only thing they have here I really want is the gym. Maybe if they shut it down, I'd have to quit coming back!

The Recreation Syndrome

MURRAY:

Working in a prison isn't all drudgery, nor is all the staff unimaginative. Actually, there are some interesting people working here. There is also a definite social life. The hideway, a local bar in town, is the meeting place for many of us. Last night I had a talk with John Bindle, the recreation supervisor here. What he had to say about his new physical fitness program intrigued me.

John is a very interesting guy. He graduated from a good state college, majoring in physical education, and had been a good athlete himself. He was a fine role model for the men: good-looking, 6'1" and 190 pounds, mixes freely with the inmates, who quickly took to calling him "Coach" after his arrival at the institution two years ago.

His ideas about corrections are simple and practical. He feels that the men are physically below par and because of this cannot do a good day's work. Consequently, they become involved with the law. He reasons that because, for the most part, the men would be released to laborer's jobs, they should be physically able to work. Like all simple, logical ideas regarding corrections, it sounds good.

When I walk into the gym this morning, I feel strange. But I always do, every time I go there. I'm not sure if this is entirely due to my unfamiliarity with gyms, or if it isn't more because of the strange way the men look at me. I know that few, if any, counselors come into the gym. The men who are working out or playing always slow their activities and talk among themselves, while looking in my direction.

As I approach John, he is his usual pleasant self.

"Hello, John," I say, matching his pleasantness. "How's the muscle-builder today?"

"Hi, melon-messer!" he answers. He calls all counselors that, even in front of the men.

"If you have a few minutes, I'd like to talk a little more about what we started last night."

"Sure," he answers, "let's go in the office where it's quieter."

His small office is just inside the main entrance of the gym, across from the equipment room and showers. The walls of his office are decorated with the usual prison scenes of inmate teams playing against outside competition, generally armed services teams and small local colleges.

"Let me tell you about the new program. Just sit down there," he says pointing to the hardwood chair across from his desk, "and I'll tell you how to cure these people."

"As each man comes in," he starts, "he will be given a physical fitness test. The test will consist of timed physical activity, such as running, jumping, chin-ups, and others which must meet a minimum standard. He will remain in the recreational program until he is able to meet that standard. He will be tested again, shortly before he leaves, to make certain that he has remained in shape. My study has shown that over eighty percent of the men are sub-standard."

"Suppose you find out," I ask, "that an inmate isn't fit when he's about to leave? What would you do, keep him here?"

"No," he laughs, "we wouldn't do that, although it might not be such a bad idea. My notion is that some of these guys wouldn't get back into trouble so quickly if they could just do a day's work. But what we would do, based on what type of job the man is going out to, is make a recommendation to the parole agent regarding his ability to perform that work. Then it would be the agent's responsibility to make a judgment on how much supervision the man would need."

"What about the men who are already seriously involved in physical activity, what bearing do you think it has on their future behavior?"

"There you go again. Most counselors treat the Physical Education Department like an orphan. They think we have leprosy or something. The only time we see any of you guys is when you're down here for a free game of ping-pong or something. You're the first counselor who's been down here in months who just wanted to talk." He pauses, and I think he has finished.

"But what about my question, John; you really didn't answer it. You're sounding like a counselor!"

"Give a man some time," he laughs. "It's just as I thought; you guys are *really* suspicious! But what I mean about physical activity and a lawbreaker's future behavior is that if he is sufficiently motivated toward exercise and participation with others, and is encouraged, he will do the same outside."

"Well, then," I continue to bait the trap, "how many guys do you actually estimate participate in a sports or recreation program now?"

It has always been my feeling that the men who really needed this activity didn't get it, and the ones who needed it the least spent their entire free time in the gym or out on the athletic yard.

"I know what you're thinking," he responds, "all that money in our budget for two professional staff and all of the expensive equipment."

"Yes," I admit, "I was thinking along those lines."

"Well, believe me, it's really necessary. When we get these guys, most of them have no idea of fair play. We even have to teach them how to *lose* a game without getting all hot and bothered. As I'm sure you realize, this is very important when we have visiting teams in from the outside. We win some of the games, of course, but when we're up against pros, or semipros, we lose most of them. You remember when we had that soccer team in from Buenos Aires? They were in this country playing professionally when I talked them into playing our men. If you didn't see it, it was a hell of a game! The guys got real excited, and we had three thousand inmate spectators! I think that's very impressive. Normally only a handful of men show up for the games. These men aren't motivated toward spectator sports, and I believe if we can do more of that we'd have a lot better success rate."

I listen, and—I guess—begin to become infected with John's enthusiasm.

"Now take judgment for example," he goes on. "Most people show some kind of good judgment. But not these guys. We first get them, and they're like children. They have to be taught, right from the basic things."

"But how about the guy," I interpose, "who is older or simply doesn't want to get involved in any physical activity? Is he left out of your plans?"

"Oh, no, we have something for everybody. For that type of person we have quiet games such as chess, checkers, and dominoes."

I don't remember dominoes as a particularly quiet game as I could recall the men slapping the hard, plastic squares down on the formica table tops in the day rooms. In fact, the discourteous domino players interfere with the men watching television, reading, and playing cards and have often become a topic in group. I have also heard stories about the extreme gambling debts, and subsequent knifings, generating from domino games. As for the chess, I remember when John arranged for the expert, Abranowitz, to come in once a month to teach the men. A couple of times a year, tournaments are arranged between interested men, and sometimes as an exhibition, the old man takes on forty or fifty inmates in simultaneous games. Only once did an inmate nearly beat him. Abranowitz has a theory about chess and criminal behavior. He feels that when one of the inmates wins a match against anyone, it is—in a sense—a substitute for overcoming a victim. He feels that if that energy which compels crime can be redirected, there would be less crime. He compares chess matches to murder. He feels that an inmate's hostility can be much more easily focused in a chess match. Everyone has a theory about corrections!

"It makes me wonder, John, what it means to have all of these games. What is the real purpose behind the elaborate gym facilities and the consequent expense?"

"You're right, it is costly, but I feel it's a justified expense."

Just as each department, I think, has its reasonable justifications, he gives me his.

"We have to have expensive equipment. We don't want the men to get hurt. Take tumbling. It's important to have good mats; otherwise there might be an injury. The same with boxing; we have to have good gloves and headgear. And the ring has to be serviceable: we can't have a rope break and risk a serious fall."

"Well," I interrupt, "take boxing as an example of what I'm talking about. Isn't it rather a specialized sport? Realistically, how many men go in for it? Or is it just used as a method of handling hostility and grudge fights?"

John laughs. He knows it is common knowledge that the coaches allow a certain number of grudge fights, as a way to avert serious trouble. And, too, grudge fights certainly draw the crowds, and raise the level of enthusiasm of the inmate spectators.

"You're partly right about grudge fights," he explains. "Only once in a while, though. Officially, we don't allow them. In practice, they seem to work. Most of the time the men are pushed into them, anyway, and it's a way to see that no one gets seriously hurt.

"But getting back to your point," he continues, "about how many guys participate in the fight game. You know, it's not how many take part in it, but what happens to the guys who do participate. I guess I'm talking about quality more than quantity."

"I'm not sure I see what you mean," I say.

"Well, take Bo Bo Brown, for instance. When he first came here, he lacked confidence. He was big, true, but we had to instill in him a feeling of confidence, the idea that being a Negro didn't make any difference. In fact, in the fight game, being a Negro might be an asset: it insures hunger and a desire for success. Look at what Joe Louis and Sugar Ray Robinson did with it. After about six months of training, Bo Bo was a different man."

That's true. They actually had Bo Bo convinced he could be a success as a professional fighter. The only difficulty was that the Parole Board didn't think the plan was a realistic one. When Bo Bo went before the Board and told them about his plans, they asked him some pretty basic questions, about past delinquent history, employment prospects if the fight game idea wouldn't work. I had seen Bo Bo that afternoon after his Board appearance, and he thought he had made it. The consequences were almost tragic. Normally, procedure calls for an inmate who has been denied by the Board to be told by his counselor. A new staff member, who didn't know about the rule, inadvertently gave Bo Bo his Board result. It read: Denied: one year.

I heard about it later. Bo Bo had been smiling when the slip was handed to him by the officer. There were about thirty inmates waiting for their results and about five staff members in the office. Bo Bo stared at the slip for a few seconds, then screamed. I guess it was more of a cry, a long, loud wail of anguish. Everyone in the office immediately froze, and then almost as if everyone instinctively knew what to do, he was left alone. I suppose also the man's size and fighting ability may have had a little to do with his being left alone. He stood for a few seconds more, than slowly turned and walked from the Custody Office toward his wing. No one followed him. I was told he was crying; it seemed odd for that massive man to cry. I remember getting extremely angry when told about it. I couldn't understand the denial.

I understood it later. Finally, after another thirteen months, Bo Bo was released. He lasted exactly two months. Then, he came back. It was the usual story. He couldn't find a job; he ran into his former delinquent companions; the squares wouldn't accept him; he was bored; the parole agent was hounding him; the police were dogging him because he had once pushed heroin—if there was an excuse for failing parole, Bo Bo had it. But what he didn't say, and what was probably closer to the truth, was simply that he had a great deal more status in the penitentiary than he did outside. Inside everyone knew him; outside he was nobody. The Parole Board was right; Bo Bo had been living in a dream world.

"I don't know, John, if that's such a good example, when you consider what he did subsequently," I answer.

"I agree," he says, "but you see my point, don't you? It is possible for an inmate to do quite well in sports. And beyond that, if you want to take another view, boxing and wrestling in prisons are essentially spectator sports. Not that many inmates participate; but approximately seventy-five percent of them attend the boxing matches." He smiles. "So you see, Bo Bo can be useful in another way."

That is, of course, one line of reasoning, to make whatever use one can of available material.

"Take the weights, for example," he goes on. "Most of the guys, at one time or another, get involved with them. With the proper supervision, these guys could really build themselves up to a point where they are certainly physically fit and able to do a day's work. Besides," he adds, "they look and feel better."

"Maybe so," I answer, "but how many of these guys are going to keep up weight-lifting? Most of them will never go near a gym after they get out. They'll be lucky if they do a half-dozen pushups in their front room, if they have a front room. More likely they'll be holed-up in some cheap hotel room, trying to outwit the bulls."

He apparently can't tell if I am serious or not.

"I don't think you mean that," he says. "Otherwise you'd be just like some of these other people here: real cynical and only interested in a paycheck."

"No," I say, "I still have an interest, but I really don't think you're being particularly realistic about these weights, for example."

John's face furrows with a frown.

"What do you mean?" he asks.

"I think the weights have other implications for these guys."

"Go on," he says, with a note of caution in his voice.

"Look over there, for instance," I continue, pointing to the weight area. "One man is straddled between two benches and another is sitting on his crotch. A few days ago I saw two men so close together that their faces were practically touching. Another inch or so and they would have been kissing." I speak more rapidly, trying to drive my point home. "I'll bet you a steak dinner that that guy on the bench has an erection!"

"Charlie, you're sick if you think that," he shoots back. But he doesn't want to take up the challenge. I suppose it would be a rather embarrassing one to prove!

"I may be exaggerating," I continue, "but not much. Look at it this way, this is an all-male society. These guys, with their muscles, are really putting on displays for each other. If most of them stayed out after they were released, maybe that wouldn't be so obvious. But you know as well as I do that the majority of them come right back. So what good are their beautiful bodies? Who are they going to show them off to? There aren't any women here!"

"I think that's ridiculous," he says. "You can't condemn a whole activity because of a high recidivism rate."

"I'm not condemning it. All I'm asking is for you to examine it in the light of what those guys are doing right before your eyes! But what I'd really like is to get them to examine *their* feelings of inadequacy. What makes it even more ludicrous is that I know at least one of those men is a hype. Sex to a hype is nothing, at least not the hypes I know anything about. Heroin is more important than women. Now what kind of kick is that? They can't have an ejaculation. And, moreover, they're caught up in a vicious circle. They use heroin on the streets so they can't or won't have to have women, and the heroin in turn keeps them in prison where there aren't any women, and around and around they go."

"I think you're getting caught up in your own analysis, Charlie. What's more, you're overlooking the value sports have for the men who have to relieve their tensions in some way."

There's another of those words again: tension! What tension? That's probably the biggest single problem in a prison—there's not enough tension. If there were more, plus lots of anxiety, there might be some change on the part of the individual man. The way it is now, why should he change? Everything's done for him.

"But how about the Southern Resort, John?"—this being my name for the minimum security institution where the men can swim, play tennis, and so on. "Doesn't that have a vague resemblance to Forest Hills?"

"I don't follow you," he says, again with that frown on his well-tanned face.

"I mean, with the inmates dressed in white shorts, tennis shoes, a towel around their necks, à la Pancho Gonzales, forgetting completely they're in a prison. Again, it's that status thing. On the outs they're not going to come within twenty feet of a tennis court, and you know it."

He has to laugh at the scene I describe, because in many ways he knows it is true.

"Admit it, John," I continue, "they opened that place in 1941, on one idea, that of giving the men more responsibility—and at the time it was a sound idea. But what happened since that time is that the original goal got lost, and it has degenerated into just another prison, sort of a 'rest-home' for the median-aged inmate who wants to do easy time."

I can't tell from his expression what he thinks about what I am saying. I didn't really mean to be so critical of his field, because I know John is very proud of his profession and sincerely feels that a well-rounded recreational program can influence a behavioral change in the men.

"Maybe you're right," he says, "about the stuff you've been saying, but I think you're all wet in the way you tie up sex with weightlifting."

"I'm not saying I'm right about anything. All I'm saying is that this is another way of looking at what I see as a problem. I think most of the men who spend a great deal of time on the weights have an inferiority complex about the size of their sex organs. I'm not saying that they have small organs, but they think they do. And a way of compensating for it is to build bigger muscles than everyone else has. Because of this poor image of themselves, they don't think they can perform so hot in bed. I furthermore think this is the main reason they keep coming back to prison, where it is relatively safe, and they don't have to deal with the pressure of having women around who might make them prove themselves."

"Man, you've flipped your lid." He shakes his head in mock sadness.

"Maybe so. All I know is guys keep coming back to prison where there are only more men, plus the fact that many of these guys like to be under the heel of authority and want to be told what to do in everything. In many ways they're terribly masochistic and have a wish to suffer. For instance, I don't think it's any accident that prisons are run by Custody in a military fashion—ye gods, man—talk about submission to authority!"

He starts to interrupt, but before he can say anything, I motion with my hand to prevent him.

"Yeah, yeah, I know, a lot of officers love their authority, but the sad thing is that so do the men. The military titles and uniforms remind the inmates they are not free and are under a rigid authority. But what makes it even more frustrating is how the counselors are caught in the middle. They are often seen as less rigid 'nice' guys because they are supposed to 'help' the inmate. They wear civilian clothes and all have gone to college and know all that 'psychology stuff.' Not only is there a gigantic split between the inmates and staff, but there is absolutely no communication within the staff—especially between Custody and Treatment. The inmates use this to their advantage and think all they have to do is 'con' the Treatment people into thinking they're ready to go out. There's so little dialogue between the staff that sometimes it's difficult to get any verification about what the inmate *really is* doing. Then they go out on parole having made little if any changes, and we act so surprised when they come back!"

"Hey," John says, "whose side are you on? Now you have me confused."

I laugh.

"I'm on my side," I answer. "I just don't think the staff knows what the hell they're doing! But I've got to go now. I'll see you later, John. I'm going to get right on it, straightening this joint out!"

Chapter 6

The
Bad Time

DUNN:

I walked out of the dayroom, where I had been in a three-handed pinochle game with Tommy and Fat Paul, onto the floor of the adjoining cell-block. I had no more than stepped out the door and stopped to light a cigarette, when close by I heard the unmistakable scuffling sounds of a fight. A fight in prison—whether you're involved or not— puts an immediate squirt of adrenalin into the system. You'd better be ready! And fast, because you can never be sure whether it's just a simple fight of if some bayonet-wielding psychopath has blown his top and is slicing every-

one in sight. I guess, too, it's a carry-over from my days in
reform school. I've been in two penitentiaries since I left
reform school, and the joints are cake walks compared to
those crime schools. For the rest of my life I'll never have
half the trouble I had in the two years I spent there.
Reform school kids' idea of a little friendly fun is a race
riot! Ever since then, I hear a fight, and I'm ready for
anything.

My first move was almost instinctively to back up to the
wall so I'd at least have protection from the rear. I quickly
looked to the left where the noise came from, then to the
right where the cellblock bull stands, to see what he was
doing. At the left there was what seemed to be the usual
aimless groupings of cons standing around. But I didn't
have to look long to see that there really was something
going on down there. The telltale sign was individual cons
quickly looking up toward the bull, then away, so they
could keep an eye on him. On the streets when there's a
fight in a bar or somewhere, everyone immediately crowds
around to watch. Not so in a joint—at least not so with the
old cons. They want to see, all right, but more important,
they don't want to rank the play by crowding around and
drawing the bull's attention. It's just the young idiots and
hoosiers who'll crowd around. The bull was talking on the
phone, so he hadn't heard anything yet.

I took a couple of casual steps toward the area of the
scuffling to at least see who was fighting. But I needn't
have bothered. For just at that minute, everyone, including
the warden at his house four miles away, heard Josiah's
scream. "I'll kill ya, ya mothafucka," he shouted.

I looked up and saw the bull slam down the phone, and
we both started running toward the noise. But I had
twenty feet on him and would get there first. There was no
doubt in my mind that it was Josiah; there's no mistaking

that nigger's high-pitched screaming. He never talks, just screams. And the only reason I wanted to get there before the bull was to see somebody kill him!

Out of the corner of my eye I saw the bull stop. He must have gotten scared because by the time I got to the fight and turned around to see where he was, all I could see was his coattails as he went flying through the corridor door.

Now everyone was crowding around, and I had to push to see who in the hell had a hold of Josiah's ass. There wasn't any need to be cool now; everybody in the penitentiary knew a fight was going on. When I finally did get to see who the other guy was, I almost had to laugh. Miller! A more unlikely guy I couldn't imagine. But even though I hated the fool, my first and most fervent thought was, "Go ahead, Miller, kill that black-ass son-of-a-bitch." At that moment, I almost liked the punk.

But in watching it for the few more seconds it lasted, it was obvious that my hope was an idle one. Neither one of them even had a weapon! So neither could have been serious. A fight doesn't last long enough in a joint. You can't waste time with your hands; if you want to hurt the guy, you got to bring something to do it with.

Josiah's threat to "kill" him seemed ludicrous. He had ahold of Miller's coat with both hands and was hanging on for dear life. He was bent down with his head in Miller's stomach to avoid the blows. If he was going to "kill" him, he'd have had to do it with this teeth! Miller was just bouncing ineffectual lefts and rights off the top of Josiah's head, and everyone knows you can't hurt a nigger by hitting him on the head!

Just then the cellblock bull and his three reinforcements came pushing into the crowd to break up the fight. I get a kick out of bulls when they have to do something like break up a fight. You can see they'd rather be fourteen other places! They act big and tough in their normal day, pushing cons around the joint. Let a little excitement happen when a con won't go for their bullshit, and they're scared to death! The only time they're brave enough is when they've got four to one odds. They've got the guts of broads.

The two sergeants and two other bulls finally got through the crowd to Miller and Josiah. As far as those two were concerned, the bulls could have gotten there a lot sooner! You could see they were relieved that they didn't have to fight anymore. The bulls didn't even have to lay a hand on them; they had parted as quickly as they saw the welcome sight of the green uniforms.

With two bulls each, Miller and Josiah were marched toward the door. The bulls were very officious, important, and silent. All of us cons were just standing around, some laughing and others talking about what a funny fight it had been. Just then we got a deluge of bulls! They must have sent up a distress signal, or pushed the panic button or something. I almost expected the National Guard to surround the joint.

The bulls were shouting, "All right, everybody to their cells," and "Let's break it up," and "All right, the fun's over for the night, boys."

When I got to the dayroom door where Tommy and Fat Paul were standing, they asked me what had happened.

"Nothing," I answered, on the way to my cell.

The
Tensions

MURRAY:

Roosevelt Josiah was in another fight last night. Every unit has its troublemakers, but it sometimes seems as though I always get the worst ones. Josiah is almost like an animal. The only thing he understands is immediate gratification of his desires. He's in more constant trouble than any other person on my case load. Every day I come to work, it's almost with the expectation that Josiah will have gotten into some more trouble during the night. This time he fought with Miller. Somehow I can't understand Miller getting into a fight with Josiah. There is obviously more to it than appears on the surface.

The Disciplinary Committee, another one of our paradoxes, meets daily to mete out 'justice' for violation of institutional rules. The Treatment staff wants to see behavior so that it can be worked with; however, Custody wants behavior rigidly controlled, hence, the Disciplinary Committee.

While walking down the corridor to keep my appointment with the committee, I begin to think what I can tell them about Josiah and Miller. Josiah will be the big problem. With his primitive qualities I am almost certain that the committee will see this latest trouble as the final straw and will want to ship him out. Miller, on the other hand, has had a few more chances in life than Josiah. To begin with, Miller is white and hadn't been locked up until he was twenty-two years old. Most men we have in prisons start a lot earlier than that. Josiah, for instance, has been intermittently locked up since he was ten. Miller, like all men here, has problems, but he has been cleared psychiatrically, which will probably weigh heavily with the committee.

When I approach the committee room, I immediately see Chuvalo and Thurlow by the door with two files in their hands. They aren't wasting any time! Walking over toward them, I try not to show my anxiety.

Chuvalo looks up at me with that smile that I now know so well.

"Well," he says, "you did it again. What's going on in that unit of yours?"

I try to be casual.

"Plenty of action, that's the way I like it," I answer. "That way, we don't get a chance to get dull, or to take things easy."

Chuvalo is about to respond, but is interrupted when Small joins us and we proceed into the committee room.

We take our seats. Chuvalo opens Roosevelt's file in front of him.

"I've already read the incident report," he begins, "and it seems pretty clear to me. Josiah started the whole thing. He's been around these joints a long time. By this time he should know better. Personally, I don't think we should waste much time with this case."

He leans back in his chair.

Small looks annoyed as he responds.

"I really don't know too much about the two involved. I've seen them around, of course—particularly Josiah—but that's about all. Can you fill me in on them, Lieutenant?"

But before we can get his diagnosis, Thurlow turns to me.

"Perhaps we had better let Charlie do that. He's most familiar with the cases. Why don't you give us a brief sketch."

Chuvalo pushes the files toward me, but I shake my head. I don't need the files to refresh my memory. Their cases are both clear-cut—at least to me.

I begin with the easiest of the two.

"Walter Miller has never known a father and mother. He was reared by foster parents with eight other siblings. It was a family without warmth. Walter never felt as if he belonged. He objected to what he saw as rigid controls set by his foster parents. He violently wanted to get away from home. When he was old enough, he joined the Navy. Because he had such poor authority models, he did badly in the Navy. He was court-martialed three times. He seems to be the type of person who deliberately sets up conditions for himself so that he will come off the loser."

I pause, look around the room to see if there will be any comments yet. Seeing no response, I continue.

"For example, he married an older woman with two children. It was another of those things people apparently do without thought, but I don't believe it. I think it was another instance of setting up failure for himself. You could say he was marrying a mother, but even that would be too simple. I think it was a hostile act. There was constant bickering in the home. It almost seems as if Miller is so used to conflict that he can't live without it. It's entirely possible that this episode with Josiah is another attempt on Miller's part to keep himself in some kind of trouble.

"There are two psychiatric reports on Miller. Let me read a few comments from each."

I motion for Chuvalo to give me Miller's file. He shoves it across the table toward me.

"The first report is written by Dr. Edward Landgan and was based on one twenty-minute interview.

"Quote, 'Subject displayed narcissistic traits coupled with patterns of sociopathy. He is unable to form any warm relationships, and he is extremely hostile toward authority. He does not learn from past mistakes. He has no conscience. I feel he is severely disturbed. Release to parole should not be considered for at least another year,' unquote."

I again look around the room, expecting some kind of response. Small apparently reads my mind.

"Why don't you read from the other report?" he says. "Then we can comment on both."

"The other report," I begin, "is almost completely opposite to Dr. Landgan's. It is a result of Dr. Landgan's and is written six months later. This one is by Dr. Bruce Woodley and is based on observations each lasting one hour.

"Quote, 'Miller does have severe inadequate feelings and he has been insecure ever since the death of his parents when he was two years old. Miller has always run from life situations. He had trouble in the Navy; he had trouble with his marriage. However, it is felt that the trouble Miller has been involved in, in the past, is a result of his trying to prove his worth as an individual. He is definitely not psychotic. He is well oriented as to place and time and has never experienced hallucinations or phantasies. He is capable of accepting the responsibility of the parole program and he should be released within the next three months,' unquote."

Small looks puzzled.

"The psychiatric reports don't really say very much, except that there is sharp disagreement between two authorities," he says.

"So what else is new," Chuvalo sneers. "I don't think we should be wasting all this time discussing Miller. As I see it, Miller's not a bad convict. He's just a victim of another of Josiah's blow-ups. Probably there's some sex or cigarettes involved. I think twenty-nine days in the hole would be good for Miller—teach him a little lesson."

I am shocked.

"In the hole," I almost shout. "We don't even know what this is all about and you want a disposition made just like that." I snap my fingers in disgust.

At my remark tension begins to build in the room. There is no longer the air of casualness. The battle lines are obviously again drawn. Thurlow looks over at me and breaks the tension.

"Why don't you continue with the description of Josiah," he says, "so we can perhaps get a better idea of what happened."

I nod in return, but take a few seconds to compose myself.

"Roosevelt Josiah," I slowly begin, "is a twenty-five-year-old Negro who is openly hostile. He has violent impulses and appears to be incapable of controlling them. He exaggerates his physical prowess and claims to be expert at judo and karate. As an illustration of his phantasies he claims to have been ping-pong champion at a state industrial school in Oregon.

"The group supervisor there, however, writes that Josiah was a mediocre player and cheated most of the time, causing the usual arguments.

"As a boy his home situation was characterized by a succession of lovers that his mother had almost nightly. Public agency reports describe the home as filthy and run-down. At one point in his life, when his mother and fourteen-year-old sister had been away for three days with men, and he had been left with no food and no money, he tried to sell some of the family furniture. It was so bad he couldn't even give it away.

"As a result of this dismal home situation, Roosevelt made his home in the streets. There at least he was able to gain some kind of acceptance and understanding. Of course, it meant that he would eventually get involved in all kinds of delinquent activity, which he began at about the age of nine. This young man has been in and out of institutions ever since he was ten years old. In the truest sense of the word, he is a child and the institution is his mother and father."

I stop talking. I am afraid if I go any further, it would only aggravate Chuvalo more.

But even at this, he wastes no time.

"So, in other words," he says, "this is another one of your hopeless cases. The well-institutionalized inmate who doesn't belong at this medium-security institution. He just wants to do time. I think we should accommodate him. Send him to the Fortress."

"No," I shoot back, "I don't think he ought to go to the Fortress. What is any kind of a prison for, anyway? If the minute a man acts out, we ship him, then what do we have treatment programs for?"

I can feel myself getting boiling mad. But I must also have touched something in Chuvalo, for he, too, is obviously angry.

"Listen, Murray," he says, "you think you're a missionary or something. If you wanted to save souls, why didn't you become a priest? I think Josiah is dangerous." His face takes on a serious expression. I can't tell if he is kidding or not. "Look at his history," he continues. "Nothing but violence and institutions. I don't see how anyone can realistically expect to do anything with this type of man. I think this is a hopeless case, and I think we had better realize it."

He now turns intently toward me. "And, Murray, I think you most of all had better realize it. Otherwise," he adds, "there'll be blood on your hands."

My curiosity gets the better of me. "What do you mean by that remark?" I ask.

"Just what I said. This guy is dangerous. The record shows he nearly killed two men when he was locked up before. On the street he was once hired to beat up someone and he practically crippled the victim. Josiah does not think about consequences. I think someday he will kill, and if something isn't done about him now because of you, you will be responsible for his victim."

"I think this is ridiculous," I say. "And furthermore, I insist that he's not a killer. Sure, he's had a messed-up life. He saw his father kill another man because of his mother. But that doesn't make him a killer. Roosevelt is a product of society and I think it's our responsibility to work with him, not send him to the Fortress where he can retreat into his dream world. If we send him there his feelings of rejection will only be reinforced."

I try to get some support from Small.

"What do you think, Ed?"

"Well," he responds, "it's true that this is a treatment-oriented institution and we are supposed to work with difficult cases, but the question is, 'Where do we draw the line?' "

He gives a perplexed gesture and continues, "The lieutenant does have a point. How much time can we legitimately expect to spend babying someone like this along, hoping that a change will take place? How many bashed heads can we afford to have? You know, Charlie, we do have the majority of the population to think about. We can't run a program for the few difficult cases."

Now it is up to Thurlow. In a sense he is my last hope. With his support, the vote will go two to two, a tie. Then it will have to be referred to a large classification meeting.

"How do you feel about it, Captain?" I ask.

He apparently realizes that his vote will be decisive and starts slowly. "I appreciate your concern, Charlie. And I agree with you that we should keep as many here as we can and work with them." He pauses, as though thinking. Now there is absolute silence in the room. We all have our eyes riveted on him.

"However," he sighs heavily, "for the sake of the institution I don't really feel that we can hang onto Josiah. I'm afraid we'll have to ship him out."

There it is. I have lost. But it isn't simply this loss that feels so overpowering; it is the cumulative effect of all the losses and countless frustrations of the past five years. Suddenly I knew I have had it! This is *indeed* it! Everyone is watching to see how I'll react.

"O.K.," I begin, throwing all caution to the wind, "that tells me where I stand around here and what kind of a phony outfit this is."

As I talk I become more and more incensed. "We say one thing and we do another. We say we're a treatment institution and yet we're always shipping people out, the minute they give us any trouble. We've got disturbed people here who act out. And what do we do with them? We threaten them with shock treatment or the Fortress."

As I pause and look around the room, it suddenly seems that they are my enemies—that these men are personally responsible for the failures and frustrations of my work. I feel myself getting almost painfully out of control. They, for their part, simply watch me, Ed with a shocked look on his face.

"We have daily group meetings," I continue. "What the hell for? Simply for an institutional device so that we can better control the men? Can anyone here honestly say that we are using the groups to try and bring about change? No. We're afraid of change, and furthermore, we're afraid of the men. We're actually cowards. And for me, I want no part of cowardice. As far as I'm concerned, either both men remain here and we work with them or I quit."

That is as clear cut as I can make it.

Ed is the first to react.

"Now, Charlie, that's no solution. You know ultimata are never practical. Let's keep talking and see if we can't work something out."

I don't respond, but I notice Chuvalo eyeing me. Perhaps he is trying to figure out if I am serious or not.

"That's a pretty dirty trick," he says, "putting your job on the line like that. You know it's hard to get counselors, and you're trying to use it. But it doesn't change my mind. You can go ahead and quit. My decision remains the same."

Thurlow raises his eyes from the table where they've been throughout my tirade. He, too, now is intently watching me. As chairman of the committee he will have to make the decision.

"I suggest," he begins, "we postpone this matter for a week and see what happens. In the meantime, we'll return the men to the unit and go from there."

At that we quietly rise and begin to leave the room. No one speaks to me as I walk through the door, but I can feel their eyes on my back while I go down the corridor. I think it is the most uncomfortable walk of my life.

Chapter 7

A
Rehash

DUNN:

I knew the next morning we'd have to rehash the fight in group. There really wasn't much to say; it was just a lousy fight between two idiots. But that wouldn't be enough for Murray. He'd want to know "why" the fight. Who in the hell could care but him?

But Murray surprised me. He didn't say a word about the fight in group. Miller and Josiah were both just sitting there, looking like the world was about to fall on them any minute. There they sat, through that whole uncomfortable group, and never a word was said about that damn fight.

It was the next day in group that the roof fell in on them. I should have known Murray had a trick up his sleeve. He's too damn slick! He'd just waited and let us lull ourselves into a false feeling of security, figuring to catch us off-balance, and then put the screws to us.

We had no more than sat down in group when he broke his usual method by being the first to speak.

"All right, Miller, what the hell was that fight all about?"

His question caught us all by surprise, but Miller most of all. The color actually drained out of his face!

"I . . . I . . . I don't know what you mean," he finally answered. "It wasn't about anything; he just bugs me, that's all."

"That's no good, Miller. I'm not buying it," Murray shot back.

In response, Miller simply shrugged his shoulders, with a disgusted look on his face. He added, "Well, that's all I know to tell you."

"O.K.," Murray said, "maybe that's all you can give us at this point, but," he added ominously, "you'll give us more than that before this group is over."

He looked around the group.

"What do the rest of you guys think?" he continued. "There were enough of you around who saw the fight. Besides, you all live together, and presumably care about one another, so someone must know what it was all about."

"I don't know what the hell you're talking about, Murray," Thomas said. "What do you mean 'we care about one another'? I don't give a damn about anyone in here."

"You'd like me to believe that, wouldn't you, Thomas? But as you know, I happen to know better."

He paused, and looked intently at Thomas.

"For instance," he continued, "this might not be such a bad time to find out why in the hell you can't stay out of prison."

"Get off my back." Thomas said. "I don't know a damn thing about the fight. Just leave me alone."

"So, that frightens you, huh? Your little, 'I don't care what happens to me,' front doesn't come across so well. Yes, Thomas, we *are* going to have to find out why you're a two-time loser. But it'll wait, we've got a lot of time to work on you. You'll be around here for quite a while."

He paused, looked around the group, spotted Josiah.

"What about it, Roosevelt," he said, "how come you're always in trouble? How come you can't stay out of trouble even in prison?"

Josiah was bent over with his elbows on his knees and his head down. He looked quickly up at Murray. His black, hostile face remained frozen. He didn't say anything and instead looked back down at the floor.

Murray looked again over the group. Everyone was watching him but no one was saying anything.

"Well," Murray said, "it's up to you guys. I don't care if we sit here all day. But I'll tell you one thing, we're going to find out what happened with Miller and Josiah."

"You're a laugh, Murray," Thurlinger said. "Now you're going to tell us what we can *talk* about. You've got us in the penitentiary, that's true, but you can't tell us what to *think*."

"I'm not telling you what to think. All I'm telling you is that we're going to be here until we talk, and I mean really *talk* about that fight."

He looked at us again—slowly, deliberately. "If this is the kind of group you guys want, that's your business. But my business is to find out about you guys. And because I'm in power, I'm going to say how it's done. As far as I'm concerned I'll send for 150 sack lunches and we'll sit here all day."

"Who in the hell do you think you are?" Price said. And almost at the same time Estrada said, "Do you think you're God?"

I was just watching Murray, trying to figure out if the guy was serious! But I knew one thing: I wasn't going to get involved in this bullshit. He really sounded like he meant it!

The regular time for the group to end was almost up. Everyone was, from time to time, looking at their $7.00 watches, waiting for the group time to be up, and I guess, to find out if Murray really meant it.

No one said anything for a full fifteen minutes. Murray just sat there, seemingly content in the silence. We were all getting anxious. Guys began to squirm around in their chairs, cough, look at their watches, and watch Murray.

The minutes kept going by, until finally, at 9:00, when the group should be over, Estrada got up from his chair and started moving toward the door.

"Where do you think you're going, Estrada?" Murray said.

"I'm going to my job, that's where I'm supposed to be," he answered.

"Not today, you're not. No one's going anywhere."

"Jesus Christ," Thurlinger said, "you can't be serious. Don't you think we got better things to do than to sit in here?"

"I don't know," Murray answered. "Personally, I don't think so."

Estrada looked disgusted, moved back toward his chair and sat down.

The silence began again. Five minutes. Ten minutes. Until finally Corici said, "What the hell do you want us to talk about?"

"I've told you; I want to know what happened between Roosevelt and Walter."

Corici looked over at Miller. "For Christ's sake, tell the man what happened so we can get the hell out of here."

"I've told you," Miller said, "the goddamn guy bugs me."

"But what were you *fighting* about?" Thurlinger asked.

"It was nothing, I guess," Miller said. "We both started to sit down in the same chair in the TV room. We had words, and one thing led to another, and we walked out into the block and then started fighting."

Estrada stood up again. "All right, Murray, can we go now? You satisfied?"

"No."

"Well, what the hell do you want?" Estrada said. "They were fighting about a chair in the TV room."

"That's not enough for me," was all Murray would say.

The silence started again. Guys began to look over at Miller. He began to feel the pressure.

"What do you want me to say, Murray?" He finally broke the silence.

"I want to know what you were fighting about, Miller."

"I've told you."

"No, you haven't."

We were all getting exasperated.

"What the hell kind of a game are you trying to play now, Murray?" someone said.

"I'm not playing any game; you guys are playing games."

We'd been in this damn group for two and one-half hours. Something had to happen soon or I'd go bugs!

"Well, Roosevelt," Murray said to Josiah, "you ready to talk now or are you still going to be like Miller?"

He looked up quickly at Murray, "I . . . I'm . . . not like Miller," he said.

"That's right. You're black."

Josiah looked like he'd been hit across the face.

"Yeah. Yeah, I'm a black man and damn proud of it."

"Are you, Roosevelt?" Murray gently asked.

"I said I am," he responded, "what the hell, you don't hear so good?"

"Tell me, Roosevelt," Murray went on as though Josiah hadn't answered, "how does it feel to be black in a white world?"

Josiah didn't answer. He simply looked at him with that baleful look which is characteristic of his face.

Murray continued to watch him. "You're not answering," he continued. "What's the matter, you don't have any feelings? Tell me, how do you feel about Miller? What would you like to do to him?"

Still no answer.

"Would you like to kill him because he's white and you're black? Is that what started it? Because all your life you've had nothing while being surrounded with people who have everything? Is that it, Roosevelt?"

Murray paused. He looked hard at Josiah. All the rest of us were watching him, too, alternating between watching Murray and Josiah.

"Is it because you've lived in filth all your life and your mother was a whore?"

"You son-of-a-bitch, Murray!"

Estrada's voice cut through the tension like a sharp knife. Everytime anybody said anything about someone's mother being a whore, some Mexican or other would get excited. I guess it's because Mexicans have got that thing going about the Virgin Mother.

Murray looked up at Estrada, then around at all of us. He didn't answer Estrada, but instead looked back toward Josiah.

It got deathly still in the room—not simply the hostile silence, but something more. I was still trying to figure it out when I noticed everyone looking at Josiah. When I turned to look at him, he was, for the first time, sitting straight in his chair, looking at Murray, and tears were running down his face!

It was damn uncomfortable there! Everyone was watching Murray, I guess for some hint as to what to do. Murray, however, just quietly watched Josiah. After a full minute, which seemed much longer, he finally spoke.

"Can you share your hurt with us, Roosevelt?" he said very gently.

I guess Josiah couldn't answer. He simply watched Murray and continued to cry.

"What the hell you doing to the guy, Murray?" Corici said.

But Murray quickly held his hand up to Corici to quiet him.

"What about it, Roosevelt?" he said.

"I . . . I . . . don't know," Josiah said brokenly.

"Sure you know. You can tell us about it."

"No, I don't know," he said, more composed now. "It . . . it seems everytime I try to do something, nothin' ever comes of it."

"Like what? Maybe if you tell us we can help you with it."

"No, nobody can help me."

"Well, like Murray says," Thurlinger said, "maybe we can try."

"Would you like to help him, Thurlinger?" Murray asked.

"Yeah, yeah, I'll help him."

"I will, too," Corici volunteered.

"Do you hear that, Roosevelt?" Murray asked. "This group is concerned about you. They want to help you."

"Well," Roosevelt said, "it was just like that fight. I've been fighting all my life, but I've never wanted to fight. It just seems like I'm forced into it. I didn't want to fight Miller."

"Then why did you?" Barnes, a new man who spoke for the first time in group, asked.

"I don't know, but it seemed like Miller wanted me to."

Everyone now turned and looked at Miller.

"Is that right, Miller?" Barnes continued.

"Yeah."

"Why?" Thurlinger asked.

Miller looked more on the spot than Josiah. He looked down, then to the side, like he was stalling for time.

"Why?" Thurlinger asked again.

"Oh," he answered, "I know no one likes me around here."

"What in the hell is that supposed to mean?" Corici quickly said.

"I mean just that. No one likes me. I thought if I did something; if I got into a fight, people would accept me."

When Miller said that it got quiet again. I was still trying to figure out what in the hell that meant when Murray spoke again.

"Maybe we've waited a long time for this kind of a group, but we might finally begin to work out some of the many problems that are in this room. Group's over; we'll meet the same time tomorrow."

Everyone got up slowly and quietly from their chairs and started walking toward the door on their way to work or school. But it wasn't like most mornings. There wasn't any kibitzing or cutting-up. Everyone seemed subdued. When I got to the door, Tommy and Fat Paul were waiting for me.

"What did you think of that?" Paul asked.

"Christ, wasn't that too much? These hoosiers'll go for anything. Did you hear the way that whole goddamned group was crying over Josiah? I thought before Murray was through he was going to have someone kiss him!"

"Yeah," Tommy said as we went through the door, "and you know what? That nigger'll be doing the same damn thing tomorrow."

A Victory
of Sorts

MURRAY:

Exactly one week later, the four of us from the Disciplinary Committee met in the same room for the same purpose.
The strain was now gone. What little feedback I'd gotten
from other employees during the week hadn't been favorable.
But today they appeared in a fairly receptive mood. It had
gone well with the group and perhaps they had heard.

I tried to be as jovial as possible when I began.

"Well, everybody, I've got some good news for a change."

There was an exchange of embarrassed laughter.

"Let's get on with your report of the meetings, Charlie,"
Ed said. "I'm anxious to hear about them."

"Well, as you might have heard, we stayed in group until the men dealt with the problem. In the end we were able to decipher what was actually happening with those two. At first there was the usual resistance. Josiah and Miller insisted the fight had been over a chair in the TV room. Most of the men in the group felt that I was trying to create a problem which didn't exist. But, following this, the whole story came out. It was the usual frustration touched off when different types of men are forced to live together."

I paused, looked around the room and had an almost over-powering urge to push the small triumph down their throats. Ever since that group I had been thinking what I would tell these bastards when we met again on this case.

But to what avail? What would it profit me to stick Miller and Josiah down their throats? I had proved that groups can be effective, and that men can resolve their problems by talking—at least to my own satisfaction. But how did they see it? Did they see it as a victory? So far everyone had been noncommital, and I didn't even have a clue as to what they thought. If I pushed what I saw as a victory, and they saw it as an accident, it would indeed be a hollow triumph. Besides, what did this victory really mean? It was an isolated incident when there were 3,700 other men, each with his own set of problems. Viewed as a total, they constitute an immense job which dwarfed this small success. Just thinking about it made me realize how little effect I have on a place like this. Each of those 3,700 men is almost a mystery. How many of them harbor violence in their heart? How many will kill someone? They're an immense threat to society, and one minimal success doesn't change the picture.

So, I thought, the best way is just to underplay it. That way I won't make anyone angry and they won't hinder me more the next time I try to do something. After all, I can't threaten to put my job on the line every time I have to have a decision made. I was lucky this time; they had gone for it.

"So, it really wasn't very much; the men were able to handle the problem. I had to do very little, it was mostly the men. Maybe if we gave them an opportunity to handle their own problems, our jobs wouldn't be so frustrating."

Chuvalo was the first to say anything. He seemed irritated; actually, I was surprised he wasn't more angry than he was. "Well, personally, I'm not convinced. You guys can bet I'm going to keep my eyes on those two. I just think they slipped through the group, but I don't want mine to be the final decision. What do the rest of you guys think?"

He looked at Small, who obviously didn't want to be put on the spot yet until he saw which way Thurlow was going to jump. So, Small, in turn, looked at Thurlow with a questioning gesture.

"I agree with the Lieutenant," Thurlow answered, "that these men should be watched."

That obviously meant that both Miller and Josiah were going to get to stay. But, of course, he had to appease both sides. His opening statement was meant to calm Chuvalo, but since I had made such a point of this case, he also had to appease me. I knew his only real concern was over the control of the inmates. He next looked directly at me and it became clear where he stood.

"I'll resolve this disciplinary report, Charlie, with only a warning and a reprimand, but that doesn't mean that I don't see the whole thing as a serious affair. In fact, it's so serious that I think you should assume responsibility for the behavior of these two men. What about it, are you assured the group can handle them?"

"Yes," I answered. "I think the *group* will be responsible for them. I see it as a group problem."

It was then that Small finally made his comments. Sure of his ground now, he put on his best smile and shook my hand.

"Congratulations, Charlie, I think you did a great job. We'll have to review this whole episode at staff meeting; we can all learn from it."

At that we all stood up and prepared to leave. Personally, I felt good; I had finally won a victory. But I also knew the feeling wouldn't last.

Chapter 8

The Goodies

DUNN:

The canteen line is always long and slow. I hate to stand in the damn thing. For that reason I try to go only once a month and get everything I need for the whole month. The worst thing about the line is that you're always a standing mark. As long as you're in the line, that means you've got money. When your friends go by and see you standing there, they always give you that con, "Hey, Jimmy, get me a box of Hi-Ho's and a jar of peanut butter and I'll catch you the next time I go to the store." But I generally refuse, saying I've only enough money for my own stuff. I make it a policy not to lend money, or anything for that matter, in the joint; it ultimately just causes trouble. If you lend a guy something, and he doesn't pay it back, that means you've got to lay a pipe across his head—and for that you can go to the hole. So it just doesn't pay to lend.

The canteen is in the main corridor. The line is always stretched for thirty or forty men down the corridor, both ways. The canteen window is fashioned like a cashier's cage in a bank. When the store is open, they remove the heavy shutters from the inside that keep it locked. The bull who actually handles your ducats and tallies up your purchases stands in the middle of this cashier-like cage which is faced with heavy wired screen; two convicts who work inside with him, and flank him on either side, take your orders. One works on each line. They stack up your purchases for the bull to check and take out the coupons from your ducat book.

Working in the canteen in the joint is a big score. The two guys who work in there with the bull get a full canteen draw, twenty-five dollars, which is put on their books. In addition, they get another full draw of twenty-five dollars worth of merchandise a month. In this way the bulls hope they'll get guys in there who won't steal. Of course, stealing from the canteen is an automatic beef, and you blow your job. They think if they make it lucrative enough, guys who work in the canteen won't take a chance of blowing their job because they stand to lose too much. But it's pretty hard to find guys in a penitentiary who won't steal, and to my knowledge, they've never gotten anyone in there who's not doing something crooked. In fact, some of the plots the bulls have uncovered for rifling the canteen would rival the Brinks job in terms of daring and ingenuity. When you get a man's attention riveted on one project, and he has enough time, chances are he can come up with a plan that would do justice to "Willie the Actor."

The corridor is the main thoroughfare of the joint, and standing in that canteen line, you get everyone and his brother running past. Everybody who passes looks over the canteen line for a likely mark. When I was in the joint the first time, I was just a kid. I had a hoosier I never saw before in my life come up to me and tell me he wanted me to buy him some damn thing. He thought he was going to scare me into buying whatever in the hell it was he wanted. But I knew from the years I spent in reform school how to get along better than that. Even though I knew he was armed, I just looked at the guy and told him to go find some other sucker. He looked hard at me for a minute, and I just looked at him as calmly as possible; then he turned and went away. I guess the memory of that kind of touchy experience is one of the reasons I hate standing in the goddamn canteen line. You never know what kind of a nut you're talking to in the penitentiary. Push the wrong button on the right guy and you've got trouble.

But as bad as I hate to stand in the goddamn thing, I'm sure glad I've got the money so I can. I don't know what I'd do without the canteen. It's rough enough simply being in the joint without being broke, too.

I had a few hundred on me when they pinched me, and that lasted me for quite a while. Then for the first six months I was in the joint, I still had that stinking broad who was sending me a hundred or two a month, and I had time to build up a little bankroll. I've got enough money to last me for about another year, but I'm beginning to worry about it. If they keep me much longer than a year, I might have to start hustling. But then I've always got my dad.

He'll see to it that I have at least cigarettes and something to eat. I sure hope he holds up for a few more years and doesn't die on me or something. But it's a bad feeling worrying about where your canteen's coming from while you're in the joint.

The entrance to the hospital is just up the corridor from the canteen line. I see guys whipping up the corridor and banging on the door of the hospital for the bull to unlock it as regular as clockwork. That goddamn hospital has more action than a Flip whorehouse. You'd think these convicts were all sick the way they bounce in and out of there.

But I know what most of them are going up there for anyway—at least why the dope fiends are going there. Old Doc Reading, who is a retired Army medical doctor, and a fish in the penitentiary, made the mistake of ordering a batch of cough syrup that has codeine in it. Every hygalow in the joint has suddenly developed a cough. They dispense it three ounces at a time. Cough syrup has a quarter grain of codeine to the ounce, so three ounces will just about give you a buzz. And clean as most of these guys are, it will do more than just buzz you. I wonder how long it will take Doc Reading and the Custody staff to snap to how much cough syrup they're dispensing for all these coughs around here. That's why I haven't been up there yet to get my little taste. I have a sneaking suspicion that as soon as they wake up to what they are doing, everybody who has his name on the list for cough syrup is going to be in a big jackpot. That is one thing I don't do in the penitentiary, consciously get myself in a jackpot.

I don't know what all those other hoosiers who aren't dope fiends are doing running in and out of that hospital. They're not going to do anything up there for you but give you a hard way to go. You gotta be damn near dead before they will make a move.

While I'm standing in the canteen line, waiting for it to open, a guy standing next to me cracks, "You going to buy any cigarettes, huh?"

"Yeah, I'm going to buy some cigarettes," I answer.

"What kind you going to buy?"

"Camels."

"You wouldn't take Pall Malls instead, would you? I got four cartons of Pall Malls that I'll let you have as a deal. I hit a guy in a Klabiasch game for more cigarettes that I can use right now, and there's some other things in the canteen I need. If you'll buy them for me, I'll give you the Pall Malls at a deal."

I don't know the guy, so I'm suspicious of him, anyway.

"No, I don't want the Pall Malls."

"Yeah? Well, O.K., if you don't want to make any money," he answers and turns around again in line.

Suddenly he turns around again.

"Say, didn't I see you in the visiting room last week?" he asks.

"Yeah, I was there," I answer.

"Did you see my old lady, man?" He looks at me intently, searching for I don't know what—maybe recognition and approval.

When I make no answer, but rather look like I am thinking, he goes on.

"That's a *fine* bitch! I don't know how you could have missed her. She was the big blonde with all that good stuff. Man, everybody in the joint, including the bulls, was looking at her."

I guess he wants me to know what a hell of a man he is. I could care less what kind of a man he is or who's coming to see him. He's still an asshole to me even if he's got Princess Margaret coming to see him.

However, he spares me the necessity of answering, for he turns around again, looking to see if the canteen is opening.

But he has a point; visits are important, to a lot of guys for a lot of different reasons. I know I dig mine, even if they are only from my old man nowadays. I'd like to get down south where you can really have some good visits; lay out on the lawn, eat that good chicken or whatever else your people bring. And if you can get a broad up there to see you, you can even get a little rubbin's.

Any of the old-time cons in the joint will tell you that visits are the worst thing you can have in the penitentiary, because they say all they do is put you on a bum kick. But I'm suspicious that the only reason they say that is because they aren't getting any visits. Generally, there isn't anybody left to visit them. But I haven't gotten that far yet, to the point I think visits are bad. I may someday, but in the meantime, I'll just keep my visits.

They finally open up the canteen and the line starts moving. So far so good, nobody's come by and put the lug on me. Must be my lucky day. Everything good must be going to happen to me today, I might even get a parole!

Finally my turn comes at the window. Man, that display behind the barred screen really looks good. Behind the convict clerk is just row upon row of all kinds of goodies. All the things the convict wants. Razor blades (the good kind, not the kind the state gives you), canned nuts, scores and scores of different kinds of candy bars and other things to eat—everything a man could want arranged in a beautiful array of mouth-watering merchandise.

I tell the con the things I want, like Jergens Lotion (we have to use that for after-shave lotion because shave lotions have alcohol in them and they're afraid we might get drunk on Mennen's), a month's supply of Camel cigarettes (three cartons, because that's all you can buy at one time; they

don't want anybody being too rich in the penitentiary),
enough Hi-Ho crackers and peanut butter to supplement
the mess hall diet so that I don't starve during the month,
and a few candy bars for intermittent treats. I pay the bull
at the center window the ducats he wants for my purchases.

I have only one more problem. Now I have to get all the
stuff to the cellblock. It's a long walk down that corridor,
and a lot of guys can yet nail me for some of my goodies.
I think to myself, "If I can only make it home with all this
stuff, I'll be safe for another month."

The Dependency Syndrome

MURRAY:

Civil Service was an attempt to rid the prisons of corruption, eliminate the politicians, and raise the standards of the employees. In a large measure it accomplished those short-range goals. But what it also created was a constipation in the system that has allowed mediocrity to become the dominant force. Creativity in the individual employee is not encouraged; in fact, it is stifled. The system has become the all-important factor, and in order for the system to survive, it must be self-perpetuating. Each employee, upon joining the system must make a personal decision. He has three alternatives. He can either work against the system and try to bring about some change, with possibly his only reward being ulcers or a series of psychosomatic illnesses; or, he can give the system what it wants and climb the ladder to an administrative position, with the resulting realization after twenty years of indoctrination that change is impossible; or, more likely, he can stay in the system, be quiet, and collect a paycheck.

As a result of this, the prison has become a haven for employees who are content with the status quo. Moreover, they become seriously threatened when a member of the staff turns against them and becomes a maverick, trying to initiate change in the system. Consequently, what has evolved is a paralyzed structure with the opposing forces complementing each other: the staff doesn't want change and the inmates don't want change.

As an illustration of the bureaucracy, the Treatment staff has a system of in-service training which means that once a week every counselor has an hour-long conference with his immediate supervisor. The idea is to help the worker discuss his professional problems in a working situation with someone more experienced. Ed Small is my supervisor. My weekly conferences with him are probably more of a hardship than of any real help.

Ed is a career man. He is forty-five years old, slightly above average height, but very slender, which tends to give him an effeminate look. This is further complicated by his very soft voice. He graduated from a state university, and later attended two years of social work school for a master's degree. When he first entered the field he was full of enthusiasm. In fact, for a few years, some of his treatment techniques were talked about at the various schools of social work. Then he went stale. Most of what he had to say now was old stuff, and there was a tendency for many of the younger workers to pass him by. They didn't laugh at what he had to say, but, more deadly, they simply ignored him.

Group treatment techniques began to evolve in prisons, partly as an economy measure, because more inmates could be treated at once. Ed's work then became even less meaningful. He presented himself in a group as the traditional noninvolved therapist. In addition, his soft appearance and gentle manner tended to threaten the men. I once attended one of Ed's small groups as an observer. The topic finally settled on how people presented themselves. The men in group talked about one another for a time, then the group shifted onto Ed. In general, the men were rather gentle with him. However, finally, one man, a huge, Irish, native Bostonian who was anything but proper, suddenly exploded.

"What do you think of Ed?" one of the inmates innocently asked Jim Norton, the Bostonian.

"I see him like a broad."

His first statement, though uttered in a normal tone, startled the group. It was when he turned to Ed that his expression changed, and it was almost as if his speech couldn't keep up with his thoughts.

He almost shouted, "You know what I'd like to do to you? I'd like to make a pussy out of you because that's what I think you are. I'd like to fuck you 'til you begged for mercy! Then I'd piss in your face and beat the shit out of you!"

The group became deathly silent: tense, uncomfortable, and maybe even a little ashamed. Norton was evidently serious. But the only reaction from Ed was that his face became a little whiter than usual. Of course, he would have to respond to the attack, or lose control of the group completely.

"Huh, huh," was all Ed said.

"Is that all you can say, you sniveling punk? What would you say if I came over there right now and slapped the shit out of you?"

For a moment I almost thought Norton was going to do it as he half-rose from his seat. I became a little anxious and wondered if I should intervene.

"Is that the way you feel about yourself?" Ed said. "Kind of angry at yourself, or angry at being in prison?"

I thought it was a reasonable response; however, the softness of his voice tended to rob the answer of any forcefulness.

Norton snarled, "I'm not angry at myself, I'm angry at you, you phony whore."

And so it went. Eventually, later in the session, Ed—after taking a great deal more hostility—was able to refocus the group and helped them interpret what the attack meant, but without threatening Norton too much. Actually, it took a great deal of skill.

I thought about that group as I entered Small's rather modest, spartan office for our weekly conference. The conferences had become another of the rituals.

"How are things going, Charlie," he said when I entered, "any problems?"

"Nothing specific," I answered, trying to match his casualness. "The usual mountain of paperwork which you and I both know doesn't mean anything."

He closed his eyes and covered them with his hand. He didn't want to get into *that* topic. It was almost a family joke around the office. Everyone knew I did as little paper work as I could get away with.

"I suppose you're right," he said. "But a certain number of records *are* necessary—you agree with that, I hope."

I had to laugh. But then I didn't want to get into it either. It was an impossible situation and certainly couldn't be resolved here.

"Actually, there's something on my mind that I want to discuss," I cautiously began.

He brightened. "What's that? A problem with one of your cases?"

That was his specialty. He fancied himself a trouble-shooter on tough treatment cases.

"No, nothing like that. It really has to do with program."

He looked puzzled.

"Program? You mean the groups, or are you having more trouble with the vocational and custody people?"

I sighed.

"That's a perpetual struggle," I answered. "And that's part of it, but only indirectly."

"This is not like you, Charlie; you're being quite vague." He appeared irritated.

"Well, I guess what I'm trying to say is that it is not something that we can settle this afternoon, or perhaps in any of these sessions. Nor is it something we can restrict to ourselves. Eventually we would have to take it to staff and if the proposal were approved, it would have to go to the state capital."

I should have known how he would react. He simply stopped listening. I could tell he really didn't hear another word I said. Change—the bugaboo of Civil Service. I actually believe he became frightened as soon as I got going on my pitch. Later, in retrospect, I knew I had made a mistake when I said "state capital." Taking things there was seen as a bad reflection on the administration of the institution, and even on Ed's own supervisory ability. Of course, he continued to respond to me; but I'm convinced he never heard another word.

He cooly asked me to continue.

"What I had in mind, Ed, was the way we deprive these guys of any opportunity to make decisions. The way we do everything for them and don't give them any responsibility as individuals. Take the laundry, for example. We have fresh laundry for the inmates three times a week. Individually, or even as a unit, the men have no part in taking care of their own laundry. Everyone outside has to see that his own clothes are clean, or at least get a wife to take care of it. Why should it be different here?"

He continued to watch me, but his expression told me nothing.

"Take the canteen as another example," I continued. "The men can draw $25.00 per month. Even the guys whose wives are on welfare can draw $15.00. No one even questions it. But I think *we* ought to take a look at it. What does it mean? Are we making things too easy for the men?"

He started to interrupt, but I stopped him before he could.

"Oh, I know the objections. If we did suddenly decide 'no more canteen,' we'd have the legislature on our necks. Some silly business about being 'democratic.' But I really do think it's unrealistic. Take inmate Dunn for an example. He gets $25.00 every month. Since his wife stopped sending it, his father sends it. I happen to know his father can't afford it. I don't know if Dunn has a hold on him or is pressuring him or what, but the money comes through every month. And then the visits. All that costs money."

"Don't you think you're getting a little overinvolved in that case?" Ed asked. "Now you're worrying about his father! I feel there may be a little transference going on there, don't you think?"

"I'm not overidentifying." I tried to recover. "I just used that as an example. I'm simply saying that we should take a look at what we're doing. When we make these guys as dependent on the institution as we do, we don't give them the chance to try out new roles for themselves. We don't really have a system of rewards. Our whole outside society is set up on the principle of rewards and punishments, yet what we give these guys in here, and in the whole prison community, becomes totally artificial."

"I'm not sure," he answered, "what you mean by 'artificial.' Don't you think we are doing the job the outside community wants us to do? They're being protected, and you shouldn't forget that's our main goal."

Christ! Sometimes he could sound so pious I felt like vomiting.

"I know that," I answered, "and my goal is the same—believe it or not. All I'm suggesting is that perhaps we might be even more effective if we could question what it is we're doing."

I suddenly had the feeling I was up against a stone wall.

"God, Ed, take a look at it! The medical and dental departments are another example. We have two full-time dentists, with four inmate assistants, two full-time doctors, plus six full-time male nurses, six inmate orderlies, and an X-ray technician—in effect, a full medical staff!"

"So, what would you suggest? That we not take care of an inmate when he is sick? What kind of a reaction would we get from the families, who are taxpayers you know, and can write to their congressmen?"

Now I was getting angry.

"That's precisely the point," I answered as calmly as I could. "We provide all kinds of services for these guys by virtue of the fact they are locked up. When they are on the outside, they probably never go near a dentist or a doctor, except in an emergency—or when some hype is trying to con a doctor for some stuff. In other words, what I'm saying is that if you *have* a full-time staff, you'll *use* a full time staff. Maybe if we used some of the money that's spent on these services for additional treatment and let them get their own dental and medical work, except for emergencies, on the outside, it would save the taxpayers a lot of money and at the same time teach the men some responsibility. It's the same principle in building institutions. If we have them, we use them. What I mean is, if we suddenly built another 3,000-man institution here, it would be full within a year. Why? Because the law enforcement agencies and courts would rather send their problems elsewhere. Instead of trying to handle the problems they create in their own communities, they'd rather pawn them off. If we didn't have as many prisons, the communities would be forced to take care of their own problems."

Now I was getting warmed up.

"I hate to keep using Dunn as an example, but I know him well, and I think he's really a product of the system. Have you ever looked at his mouth? Every cavity in it is solid gold! Plus, he has an upper bridge of gold. I asked him about it, and he told me it was done here. I happen to know that the going price for that kind of job is twenty cartons of cigarettes for the inmate assistant. Can you imagine? Christ, he has better dental work than I can afford! Something like that you or I'd pay $1,000 for—this is the kind of thing I'm talking about."

I hoped that my point would be clearer now. It wasn't. Ed shook his head.

"It seems to me that you are reacting to the general frustration of the job, the excessive paper work, which you admit is tedious, and the impersonality of a large institution. I really don't see your point about a cutback in services. I am ready to admit that these services do help us run a smoother institution, but that is only a secondary gain. The smooth institution is mostly to appease the outside community. They don't like prison riots. It's the outside community that wants to be protected from these guys, but they also want us to be quiet and efficient about it."

There it was: that stone wall again.

"I'm not saying, Ed, that we shouldn't want to run a smooth institution. But that can become a goal in itself, and other things tend to be forgotten. I agree, there's no virtue in having turmoil in an institution just for the sake of having turmoil. But I am asking that each department, including counselors, take a look at what they are doing within the framework of the institution. Maybe we can discover a better, more effective method of helping people to change. The way it is now, we have all this authority over these guys, and we exercise it in such a way that it is impossible for the men to make any kind of a decision about themselves."

"I'm afraid you're still not making yourself clear, Charlie."

"All right, I'll try again. What I meant about authority is that I realize many of the men want it, and it may be the reason many of them are here. Their surrender to us of the authority they should have over themselves is really an escape for them. By our excessive control, we fall into their trap. And at the same time it makes us feel good, and we con ourselves that we're bringing about some change."

"Now you are confusing," he said.

"O.K., then, let's say, for example, that we asked the men to help us run the institution. Of course, we should know that the men run the institution anyway. But I would ask them to help us run it in a different way, with our help. They could take part in the administrative decisions, as long as we felt the decisions would be of real value for the men. Naturally, we would make mistakes, but we have to allow mistakes if they're going to learn. It would be more of a 'we' concept, rather than the present 'we-they' business."

I sensed that Ed was getting impatient. He glanced at his watch, perhaps wondering when the hour would be up.

"Take the visiting privilege for another example," I continued. "Under the plan I propose, visiting would only be done in the large group, with all of the inmates present. This would serve a dual purpose. First, the group and the staff could get a real understanding of what kinds of problems are going on in the families. We could at least know what the problems are so we could work on them. Secondly, we wouldn't get the distorted, one-sided picture the inmate presents of his family relationships. For another thing, the families would get a chance to see how the inmate really operates in the institution, what *his* immediate problems are, and also an understanding of what institution life is like. The way it is now, the families get an entirely unrealistic view of an institution. The visiting room, with its upholstered chairs and deliberately fostered 'fun-loving' atmosphere, accented by rows of coffee, cola, candy, and cigarette machines, simply doesn't give a true perspective of a prison. There would be no such thing as weekly visits alone with the families. We might make allowances for special emergency visits, but only rarely. With such a system, we'd have tighter controls, but not in a negative sense. It would enhance treatment prospects by the absence of confidentiality and family secrets; it would force the inmate to deal more with the world of reality and less in his world of fantasy."

I stopped, expecting *some* kind of a reaction to my plan from Ed. When nothing was immediately forthcoming, I continued, "If you'd like, Ed, I'll have this plan written up in proposal form, and after you've had a chance to evaluate it, we can take it to a general staff meeting."

Ed took a moment to answer, and I thought he looked tired. Actually, when he did respond, it was in such a general manner, it was almost as if he hadn't heard anything I'd said.

"Charlie, you've expressed a lot of good ideas. Some of them, I suppose, we could eventually put into practice when the administration is ready for them. Others, probably not, because of situations beyond our control."

I wasn't exactly sure what he meant. Cautiously, in order to be sure, I asked, "You mean you want me to go ahead and write the proposal?"

"Hold on. I didn't say that. I think the ideas will have to be explored in a number of conferences much more fully before they'll be ready for such a step."

"Of course, I understand that," I responded, "but things have a way of bogging down around here. I'd be willing to put in some of my off-time to begin the preliminary work; then we could perhaps meet a few evenings at your home to finalize it."

"Yes," he said, "I suppose we could do that sometime, not for the next few weeks, however; I have family visiting, and you know what that means. I don't like to discuss business with relatives around."

"I'd invite you to my place, except I have few living conveniences and, of course, we can't drink on the prison grounds."

Another one of the many inconsistencies about life around a prison. Staff, if they live on the grounds, could not have alcoholic beverages in their quarters. Yet everyone knew this rule was constantly broken.

He tried to end the interview.

"Why don't we just leave it at this, Charlie? I'll see if I can't budget some time, and we can get together and talk."

Misunderstanding him, because I thought (or hoped) the only problem was someplace to meet, I suggested we rent a motel room over a weekend.

He tried to smile—and suddenly I began to get the idea. He simply didn't want to meet with me.

"I appreciate your enthusiasm," he said, "but I don't like to mix my private life with my professional life. The children need me at home. I don't see enough of them as it is. What with the P.T.A., church meetings, and other things, I have very little time."

It was getting clearer all the time. I decided to make one last attempt. "Well, Ed, if you don't have any time to discuss it further, may I have your permission to take this up directly with Mr. Cokely?"

That really touched a button.

"No," he angrily replied. "Definitely not and I absolutely forbid it."

Now *I* was really angry, but tried to hide it as best I could. "The thing that bothers me most, Ed, is what happens to ideas around here."

He suddenly became conciliatory.

"I didn't mean to sound sharp, Charlie, but I do think you might be pushing things just a bit too hard. I know you're very much involved, and we certainly appreciate the extra work you do. But change in institutions comes slowly. Change has to be evolutionary, rather than revolutionary."

He smiled broadly at me, which only incensed me more. He was caseworking me!

He gathered papers into neat piles on his desk, the signal that I was to go. I realized that I had lost this round, but I was determined to see if I couldn't work around it some other way.

"Well, maybe we can pick it up again next week," I said, rising. "If not then, perhaps later."

"Sure, Charlie," he said. "We'll get together on it. I feel certain we can work out something."

He smiled again.

"Same time next week then?" I asked.

"Certainly. Keep up the good work, Charlie."

I could go now. The bureaucratic machine was satisfied.

Chapter 9

The Ordeal

DUNN:

Something's going on and I'm not sure what it is. Somebody's got some plans for me, but I can't find out what. That's the trouble nowadays, since they changed from having inmate clerks work on confidential material, you can't find out anything. All the casework and record keeping is done by free personnel. I scouted around and asked everybody I thought might be able to find out for me, but so far I've drawn nothing but blanks.

Two days ago I had an interview with Dr. Palow. It was a funny interview. He's a strange duck; for the most part he just sat there and looked at me for the twenty minutes I was there. The few questions he did ask me were nonsense things having to do with what's going on in the joint. He didn't ask me a word about the streets. I played the same game with him and just sat there and watched him, answered his questions as briefly as I could, and we saw who could outstare the other.

But still something's going on; I know it is. This morning I got a ducat and all it said on it was "To the Classification Committee." But I haven't put in for a job change, and I know they're not planning to change my custody, so I can't figure out what they want me in classification for. Besides, today isn't even classification day.

But I'm sure something's going on, there's something in the works for me. I'm still trying to figure out what that talk with Palow was all about. I know I'm getting short for the Board, less than thirty days now. The only guys who have to see the psychiatrist before they go to the Board are guys with real violent beefs, or sex beefs. And I'm here on a nothing charge—a common second-degree burglary. The same as at least a third of the guys in the joint. They don't have to see the psychiatrist. So that means something—I'm not sure what—but at least they're thinking about me. And it does mean there's something in store for me. I've been here three years now almost, so I'm glad at least they know I'm in this goddamn penitentiary.

When I show up for my ducat at ten o'clock like they told me—to the so-called Classification Committee—I go through the corridor and ask Fat Paul what's going on. He says he doesn't know, but the big shots are in the back. I feel a little uneasy because there are no other convicts in the waiting room. That means the big shots are here to see me, and I can't figure out what I have done lately to make them take such an interest. When the buzzer sounds and I go into the room, I know right away I'm in some kind of trouble.

They all are there: Palow, Chuvalo, Small, and Murray. All I can think if is, "All right, Jimmy, this is it. Be careful 'cause they're after you now!"

Murray gives me that noncommital look of his and starts it off.

"Good morning, Jimmy, have a seat. We want to talk to you about your progress here and how you're getting along."

I know when dealing with these whores to say as little as possible. "All right," I answer. There's not too much they can get from that!

My old friend Chuvalo flips through my file and says something smart about my only being involved in one disciplinary report. That sarcastic son-of-a-bitch!

Small, in his wishy-washy way, starts questioning me. But their methods are so obvious it hurts. So we just spar around for a while longer until Palow says something about "evaluating" my *threat* to the outside community.

While I'm thinking about something to say to Palow, the turd, Chuvalo, gets that look of his, with the dead Indian face, and asks me about a swindle I had gotten into with a trick. My first thought is, "Oh my God! You mean that's what it's all about? What the hell am I going to tell these people?"

"Well, if you're talking about that fight I was in, that whole thing was exaggerated."

"I guess that depends on what you mean by exaggerated," Dr. Palow says. "The victim *was* pretty badly hurt."

Yeah, it's getting real clear now. These whores are going to let me out of here. They're just trying to find some reasons to do it.

But what am I going to tell them about that scuffle where I had to dump that hoosier? I can't tell them the truth. I don't have any choice but to stick to the same story I gave the bulls.

*   *   *

What really happened was that my old lady was working calls in the city. One afternoon we were lying around in the apartment when about two o'clock she got a phone call. The guy was juiced and wanted to come up to see her right away. We needed the money—besides it's bad policy to turn down tricks; their feelings might get hurt when they can't even get laid by a whore. So, she told him to come on up. After he had hung up, she told me she had never had him when he was drunk. She wasn't too sure how he'd act and asked me to stick around in case she had some trouble. We both took a big geeze before he came, and I dragged a chair into the big front hall closet, turned off the lights, put my feet up on the bureau in there, and went on the nod. I don't know how much time went by, but I woke up later and heard her calling my name and some scuffling going on in the front room.

When I came down the long hall and turned the corner into the front room, this asshole was lumping her up over in a corner of the room. She had on a black lace, shortie nightgown and high heels, and he just had his pants on. He had her crouched down in the corner, with her hands over her head, trying to protect her face. He was taking long, loping, overhand shots at her. I don't know whether they had fucked yet—it never occurred to me to ask her later—but he had already messed her up pretty bad and kept on beating the hell out of her.

He didn't know I was there; he was so drunk that he hadn't heard me when I came into the room. It was an easy matter to come up behind him, especially with him so intent on his work, take his right arm and run it up his back. At the same time with my other hand, I grabbed him by the hair and snapped his head back, then started running him for the door.

But for being drunk he reacted pretty quickly. When I was waltzing him by the low coffee table, where my old lady had a fancy wine bottle with a single rose in it, he grabbed the bottle by the neck, half-turned, and hit me over the head with it before I realized he even had it.

He'd hit me on the left side of my forehead, with just enough force to stun me. When the bottle broke the shattering glass made a few little cuts on my face. It just stunned me, not enough to knock me out, but just enough to make me let go of him. I was kind of dazed then, but I did hear my old lady hollering, and I looked up just in time to see the busted end of that bottle coming, in an overhand arc, toward my face. I pulled my face back and it just caught the end of my nose, cutting that pretty badly, and in the follow-through, it cut my left arm deep on the bicep. It's a good thing my old lady is a game broad, because she really saved the day for me. She grabbed the end of that broken bottle he was waving, cut the hell out of her hand, and hung him up just long enough for my head to clear.

While he was half-wrestling with her for the bottle, I got in close to him, grabbed him by the neck with both hands so he couldn't swing clear at me with the bottle, and drove a hard right knee into his groin. I didn't really get his nuts, because he didn't go down. I hurt him enough to slow him down so I got a right hand in that did knock him down. I must have went a little berserk then; the next thing I remember was that my old lady was pulling on me and screaming. I had kicked him eight or nine times, and they told me later I had broken a few of his ribs.

But the lousy son-of-a-bitch, we were the ones who got hurt! All we were doing was minding our own business in the first place 'til that drunken hoosier had to mess up our whole day. In fact, he put both of us out of action for two weeks. She sure couldn't work much with that bandaged hand—tricks don't like to pay for spoiled pussy—and I looked like I'd been through a meat grinder.

After I stopped kicking him, I just grabbed his arm, dragged him down the hall, out onto the landing, and dumped him down the stairs. When I went back into the house, it was some scene! I was bleeding all over the damn place from the cut on my arm. My old lady was bleeding like hell where she cut a small artery in her hand, and blood was spurting all over. She was running around the apartment smearing the joint with blood in a kind of hysterical way. I grabbed the rest of that fool's clothes and threw them down the stairs after him.

I really didn't think the son-of-a-bitch would call the bulls, but that's how squares are. They get hurt—it doesn't matter what they did that caused them to get hurt—and the first thing they think of is calling the police.

About an hour after I threw the bum down the stairs, two blue suits knocked at my door and took us to jail. I had only just gotten the blood stopped from my old lady's hand and my arm, and gotten the place cleaned up a bit. Neither my old lady nor I would tell the bulls anything about what happened, so I really don't know what the damn police report said. All I know is after two weeks in jail, they cut us loose. I never went to court on it or anything; the charge they had me booked on was assault with a deadly weapon. But after two weeks they finally told me that the guy wouldn't press charges (he must have thought better of it when he sobered up), and they didn't have enough evidence to press the complaint themselves. So I just forgot about the damn thing, and now it shows up four years later to haunt me.

*   *   *

What the hell am I going to tell these hoosiers now? I can't tell them the truth because a pimp is a bad word to these guys.

"Well, what I mean by exaggerated," I answer, "is that the guy said something to me that I didn't understand. So when I asked him, somehow we got into a scuffle, and he fell down the stairs. That's when he got hurt. I didn't hurt him."

"You really believe that, Mr. Dunn?" asks Dr. Palow.

"Sure, that's what happened."

"In other words," Lieutenant Chuvalo says, "the police reports are lying, is that it?"

Everybody is looking angrily at me now. Jesus Christ! I can't tell these assholes the truth, and the lie comes out so unconvincing it even sounds bad to me.

"Well, I don't know if they're lying," I answer. "I've never seen the reports. But if they say too much differently than what I've said, something's wrong."

Dr. Palow, losing the psychiatrist's objectiveness, says, "Suppose we told you we believe the police reports, and that they are quite different from your version. Then what?"

Christ, I have no choice but to keep going now. "I don't know how I could convince you."

Dr. Palow looks around disgustedly at everyone else. "Well, I've nothing more."

I want to say some more because I know that this hasn't gone well for me at all. But then I think about it and decide I better leave well enough alone. Murray has been intently watching me the whole time.

"Well, that's about all for now, Jimmy," Murray says. "I'll see you back in the unit."

I get up and get the hell out of there, before anything more is said. I have a real sinking feeling. Now I don't know whether they are going to let me out or not.

The Challenge

MURRAY:

When each inmate enters the prison system he is subjected to three months of intensive scrutiny and testing. It is an effort to evaluate a man and how he will perform, both in prison and after he is released. Because each new arrival is an unknown commodity, Custody and Control demand excessive security until all tests have been completed at the Diagnostic Center. Diagnosis and prognosis: fancy words for what it is thought a man is like, what he might do, and how he sees the world about him. What

often happens is that great emphasis is placed on psychological profiles, which in themselves—because of our limited
knowledge—are questionable. However, we place a childlike
faith in them and act as if there is little margin for error.
We proceed on the premise that the evaluator will, at all
times, remain completely objective and not allow his own
feelings and moral judgments to interfere in interpreting the
behavior or past of the inmate.

The inmate's entire stay, and how he is treated in the
prison system, is predicated on the basis of that early
evaluation at the Diagnostic Center. It is only in rare cases
that further evaluations are made on an individual inmate.

                        *   *   *

For a number of reasons, Dunn became one of the rare
cases. Both times he entered prison he was evaluated by the
Diagnostic Center as a passive-aggressive sociopath with
strong dependency needs. This evaluation was based on two
projective tests, the Rorschach and the Thematic Apper-
ception Test; one personality profile, the Minnesota Multi-
phasic Personality Inventory; an IQ test; interviews with a
psychologist, psychiatrist, sociologist, vocational counselor,
and chaplain; and complete physical and dental checks.
Both times he was seen as the same, with no change having
taken place between convictions.

According to the psychologist, Dunn had a lot of anxiety
about inadequacy as a male, and he attempted to find
substitute phallic symbols. The needle in the arm was seen
as an example of this. There also were indications about
doubts as to how powerful he was as a man. This would
explain his emphasis on muscles. It was almost as if he
were shouting to the world that he was a man. The interpretation was that Dunn was attracted to objects that he

viewed as masculine—powerful cars, guns of all kinds. The Rorschach definitely indicated that he did not give the normal amount of responses. The average educated male gives around thirty-five responses; Dunn could only come up with thirteen. The inkblot figures did not mean much to him, indicating repression which would prevent him from responding.

In the three years that Dunn has been back on this present charge, he has managed to upset quite a few staff members. Actually, I was hard-pressed to understand why. Dunn was the model inmate; he never broke any of the rules, didn't talk back to staff, and managed to get good work grades. Perhaps it was his withdrawn, nonchalant attitude. Anyway, Dr. Palow, as a result of his interview with Dunn, prior to his Board appearance, initiated a special staff meeting to discuss what he saw as Dunn's possible violence potential.

Of course, I could understand the department's concern in trying to isolate the possible violent offender; however, I felt there was inherent danger in the use of this kind of label; there was the possibility of a mistaken diagnosis, and it could set up negative expectations for the inmate. For instance, if Dunn were to be labeled "high violence potential," regardless of the possibility of mistake, he might become violent to meet this expectation.

Sitting in my office, thinking about the coming meeting on Dunn, I felt that there was an equal possibility the committee would choose one of three alternatives. One, they could decide that Dunn was really not dangerous, and leave him where he is; two, they could finally classify him as a "hopeless case" and transfer him to the Fortress; or three, they could decide that he needed additional treatment and transfer him to the hospital for violent offenders. Actually, I think Dunn could handle the latter quite well.

He could charm the middle-class psychiatrists and psychologists by coming up with the right answers.

Personally, I didn't see Dunn as a violent type; that is, unless deliberately provoked. Goethe said that everyone has the seeds of murder within them. But Dunn wouldn't act on it without being pressed beyond his limits. There are, of course, countless women in the world asking to be punished, and one might likely push Dunn too far. It's my feeling that most people who are punished, or even murdered, in a sense ask for it. But I wondered how I could convey this idea without upsetting the committee.

This whole process is a definite fault in the system. On the one hand, the inmate's whole stay is based on an initial diagnosis, done when, of course, the man is under tremendous pressure. On the other hand, future decisions, like the one planned for this morning, present another kind of dilemma for the inmate. If Dunn seemed too hostile, he would upset Dr. Palow; if he seemed too passive and conforming, he would be accused of "doing time" by Chuvalo; and if he sounded too healthy, the Treatment staff would get suspicious.

In any case, I felt I would go to the Classification Committee and see what I could do to keep Dunn here.

When I walked into the familiar committee room, where all important decisions are made, I was happy to note that Thompson and Sansome would not be part of the meeting. Their rigidity would have only served to further isolate Dunn. I greeted Palow and Small, nodded to Chuvalo, and took my seat.

Palow started, "We might as well get this over as quickly as possible. I have some additional cases to see."

Chuvalo responded by pressing the buzzer that would bring Dunn into the room.

When Jimmy walked in I noticed that he quickly took stock of the committee, probably sizing them up, and when I motioned toward the end chair, he sat down.

"Good morning, Jimmy," I said, "we want to talk to you about your progress and how you're doing. I think you know everyone on the committee, don't you?"

He answered quickly, "I'm getting along all right." Too quickly, I thought. It would probably be interpreted by Palow as hostility.

Chuvalo leafed through Dunn's file, suddenly stopping at one page.

"I see you only have one disciplinary report. Not much for a guy that's been here three years." He slowly smiled at Dunn, "I guess you really know how to do time?"

There it was again: if a guy kept his nose clean, they said he knew how to do time. If he caused trouble, then he was a recalcitrant. Where did an inmate learn to be an inmate? By what special process did he learn to please the many different staff members, each with his pet idea on how an inmate should respond? I suddenly had the distinct impression that this was going to be a more difficult meeting than even I had imagined.

Dunn looked at me briefly, then turned back to Chuvalo. I wasn't sure if he was asking for help or not.

"I guess so," he responded to Chuvalo, though not answering the smile.

Small moved in to try another tactic. His approach was the "friendly-father" one. "Tell us, Jimmy, what you've been doing since you've been here."

Good God! I hoped he didn't really say what he'd been doing here. I was certain it would be enough to get him sent to the Fortress!

Dunn looked Small straight in the eye.

"You know that better than I do. It's all on those papers there in front of you."

"That's not exactly what we mean," Small said. "I see you're working as a hall porter. Do you plan to be a porter on the outside? We want to know what you have in mind for yourself."

I couldn't help feeling that if Dunn really answered that question, we'd be horrified. I was certain that he'd made the decision that he simply wouldn't work a forty-hour week and would instead take his chances.

However, in responding to Small he seemed to soften a bit. He almost sounded sincere.

"No, I know I'll make it this time. I'll go back to tending bar and mind my own business. I don't want any more of these joints."

I wished he hadn't said that. He couldn't have given a more trite and expected answer if he'd tried! Every two- or three-time loser said that as he kept coming up before the Parole Board. It was almost a death knell as far as getting a parole was concerned.

Palow looked at Dunn with interest. "I'm not sure that prisons are necessarily the answer for people in trouble. They don't seem to have helped you much."

I wondered what Palow was leading up to. I could sense a trap in the academic question, but I wasn't sure. Luckily Dunn made no response, simply looking at him as though a response wasn't called for. What he could say, however, would probably have filled a book!

Not getting a response, Palow continued, "Could you tell us about some of your past behavior and why you've been in so much trouble?"

"So what's to say? I don't know. I've just gotten into a lot of trouble."

I suppose that answer was as safe as any. In a way, how could Dunn really know? If he did know the reason, and continued to get into trouble, he could be classified as a psychotic.

But his answer did accomplish one thing; it certainly angered Chuvalo.

"You mean," he almost snarled, "that's all you can tell us about your behavior when you beat that man half to death?"

Now the trouble would begin. I knew it would come up. I also had been interested in the unproved, though highly suspicious attack Dunn was apparently involved in last time he was out. But my interest was in trying to get him to talk about it in group in an effort to examine what the behavior meant. Chuvalo's interest was only to punish him for it. To date, Dunn had yet to say anything about it to anyone, as far as I knew.

That, I guess, was the problem: the mystery surrounding the attack.

Dunn slowly answered, "Well, if you're talking about that fight I was in—that whole thing was exaggerated."

I felt Dunn was lying, but I didn't want to get involved in an argument at this point, for it would only serve to further Chuvalo's purpose.

But Palow interrupted, "I guess that depends on what you mean by exaggerated. The victim was pretty badly hurt. Perhaps part of the reason for this meeting is to evaluate your threat to the community for the future."

This, suddenly, became the crucial turning point of the meeting. The issue was now crystallized. Either Dunn is dangerous or he is not. Everything would depend on his next answer.

Dunn took a great deal of time in responding. Before he actually said a word he went through many time-stalling devices. He smiled at Palow, as though to gain his confidence; pulled his chair closer to the table, to indicate his sincerity; and started.

"Well, what I mean by exaggerated ... is that the guy said something to me that I didn't understand. So when I asked him, somehow we got into a scuffle and he fell down the stairs. That's when he got hurt. I didn't hurt him."

I wondered if Dunn really believed his own story. He certainly said it convincingly enough, but I, for one, couldn't believe it. "Too pat" was the only thing I could think of.

Palow looked incredulous and responded accordingly. "Do you really believe that, Mr. Dunn?"

"Sure, that's what happened."

Chuvalo beamed, triumphantly. "In other words," he said, "the police reports are lying. Is that it?"

"Well," Dunn quickly responded, "I don't know if they're lying; I've never seen the reports. But if they say too much different than what I've said, then something's wrong."

By sheer, fortunate happenstance, Dunn hit at his only salvation. The staff is never convinced that police reports are one hundred percent accurate.

Palow, however, stuck to his point. "Suppose we told you we believe the police reports, and that they are quite different from what your version is. Then what?"

Dunn shrugged his shoulders. "I don't know what I could say to convince you."

Palow turned to the rest of us, resignedly raised his hands in a gesture of futility. "Well, I've nothing more," he said.

Actually I was grateful that not much had been accomplished. At least Jimmy would not be transferred in the near future. It would give me additional time to work with him.

Now that the iron was hot, I quickly intervened to close the meeting. "Well, that's about all for now, Jimmy, I'll see you back at the unit."

Dunn seemed reluctant to leave. But I wanted to get him out of there before he got himself into further difficulty. I motioned for him to leave.

Dunn had no more than left the room when Chuvalo angrily said, "You see what we have there—a hopeless case!"

"I'm not sure what you mean, Lieutenant," I answered.

"Don't try that 'group' stuff on me. You know what I mean. That son-of-a-bitch is dangerous and here we are pussy-footing around with him as if we were walking on a crate of eggs."

I think Chuvalo was more angry than I had ever seen him. I attempted to pacify him. "All I'm saying is that we really don't know that much about a guy like Dunn. It's true, he's smooth—and perhaps even dangerous. But we have no real evidence, and because of that we have to be careful how we use labels."

I looked to Palow for some support, as I'd often heard him advise against using labels, but this time he simply sat quietly.

Small, however, intervened.

"I agree with Charlie. I think we should be extremely careful how we use labels. If we say Dunn has 'high violence potential,' then everyone who comes into contact with him will expect him to be violent."

Again I looked at Palow, expecting him to agree, or even to disagree. But he continued to say nothing; it was almost as if he'd completely washed his hands of the whole affair.

When no one else seemed to want to end the meeting, Small made a suggestion.

"Charlie, you seem to have more of a relationship with Dunn than anyone else. Being on your case load, you can watch for any gradual changes in his attitude. Really, at this point, I think we should leave it in your hands."

"Suits me fine," I responded, "how about a reevaluation in three months?"

At that the committee broke up. But as for me, I felt it was over. I had the distinct feeling that it would never be brought up again. Things have a way of dying in prison.

Chapter 10

The
Parole

MURRAY:

Maybe I've been working here too long. It's getting to be discouraging to feel that you work hard, and somehow there isn't much to show for it. The men continue to fail and come back to prison. It seems almost an insoluble dilemma. We tell the men that freedom is important, but they make it clear they've condemned themselves (and far more effectively than any court of law) to a prison existence.

Dunn is coming in this morning for his pre-Board interview, and I can't help thinking, "What the hell does it mean?" So, I write Dunn's parole evaluation, the Board reads it—but then what? I'm pretty sure they'll base their decision, not on what I say in the report, but on factors quite irrelevant to the situation.

Actually, though it's little realized, the real maker of prison policy is the community at large. When the community becomes unreasonable about a subject, as they are now about the so-called "narcotic menace," it only serves to make prison programs more and more restrictive, and the chances for effective change less and less. Perhaps narcotics do constitute a menace; I'm in no position to judge. But I do know that statistics show there are considerably fewer addicts today than there were fifty years ago, and there is a growing body of evidence to support the notion that it's not a legal and moral problem, but rather a medical and psychological one. Because the politicians respond to the public's fear, it means that prison workers are shackled in attempts to find more practical solutions to the problem.

And then there's the ethical question. Dunn is a good illustration. He really hasn't changed much to warrant a parole if one were to use the concept of change as the measure. All I can say in the Board report is that he is an excellent worker and gets into little trouble. But can I, therefore, justify keeping him here simply because he hasn't made the changes that are expected? The ethical question is, can he be kept here when the system really hasn't allowed him to change? In fact, the system has discouraged change.

*   *   *

That was my thought when Dunn walked in. I smiled at him, perhaps out of embarrassment, as he handed me his ducat. There was no sense speculating about what might be done with him. Here he was now and something had to be done immediately. Actually, I saw no alternative for myself but to try to get him out on parole. The agent then could see what he could do. He had his little book of rules, and if Dunn didn't follow them, he'd be back here.

"Sit down, Jimmy," I said, "it's that time of the year again."

He only smiled in response.

"We'll talk about what you've been doing," I continued, "since your last denial."

"O.K." he responded.

We got down to business. "I see you only had the one disciplinary, two years ago. The Board will be impressed with that; they don't like troublemakers."

"That's good," Dunn said. "I could use some help."

It was odd that you so often hear in prison the words "help" and "trouble." The inmates say they want help, and the staff tells them to stay out of trouble. Somehow these two notions get corrupted. I doubt whether the inmates really want help; nor am I sure the staff really wants the inmates to stay out of trouble.

"You've been a hall porter for two years—that may not be too good for the Board—that's not much of a job—and especially if you come up before Mr. Hinsley. He used to be a counselor at this institution. Did you know that?"

Which meant that Hinsley would know exactly what Dunn had accomplished in the two-year period. I happened to know that Hinsley was a bug on vocational training and education. The only hope was to stress what Dunn had learned in group about himself as a person.

Dunn looked up at me in disgust. "Yeah, I've heard," he answered.

"There's not too much we can do to minimize that," I went on.

Actually there'd been a total lack of involvement on Jimmy's part in the group program. I didn't feel I could tell outright lies, but how was I going to get him out of here when I felt he'd been on vacation for the past three years? "You can't look too good as a hall porter. How come you didn't keep on with the welding when you first came here?"

"I already have a trade," he responded. "I'm a bartender."

"I see your work grades are at least good. Officer Brown says you're an excellent worker; I'll have to incorporate that into the report."

I looked closely at him. "What about church? Do you go to church?"

I was hoping he'd at least lie and say yes. Then I'd have something to put into the damn report.

"No," he said quietly.

I switched topics, hoping to get something I could say about his family ties. "Have you heard from your wife since the divorce?"

"Not directly," Dunn answered quickly. "But I heard from other people she's doing all right."

I wondered what he meant by "all right."

"Do you think there's a chance of a reconciliation? This is probably one of the questions the Board will ask."

"No chance," he answered emphatically. He seemed to be definite enough about that. Perhaps the Board would take it as a sign that he could at least make a decision.

"I guess," I continued, "all we have to do now is explore a bit of the things you've learned about yourself since you've been here. We have to give the Board something to release you on, if that's their intention."

I hoped I wasn't encouraging him too much. I didn't want him to raise any false hopes in case I couldn't swing it so he could get out.

"I've learned a lot about myself," he responded. "I've gotten a lot of insight."

So he'd gotten insight. What insight? He'd been a hall porter for two years. Had this helped him to find out why he kept coming back to prison? He really didn't know. But, again, was that a reason to keep him here?

"Listen . . . I think I know what you mean by that, but if you say that to the Board, if you say that to Mr. Hinsley, he's going to ask you what you mean."

Not only that, he was going to tear him apart—rip him up into little pieces—and throw him back into the yard for another year.

I didn't know if Dunn had heard me or not, because he responded with, "I think it's the divorce that really changed me—that really made me stop and think."

Christ! How could you deal with that? What the hell was I going to do? It seemed hopeless. The only thing I could bank on was that I would be in the Board room with him and maybe I could help him through it.

"O.K., Jimmy, we'll see you at the Board."

I took his ducat, signed it, and he left.

After he left I sat there, struck by that overpowering feeling of hopelessness. What were we doing here? What was our goal? Rehabilitation or punishment? If it was rehabilitation, it meant that we had to teach men how to live again. But could we do that here? After he got out he couldn't vote, he couldn't drive a car, or get married without permission; in fact, he could hardly live normally— unless he got permission! If it was punishment, I wasn't even sure we were doing that.

The
Cut-Loose

DUNN:

The Game: End or Beginning?

   This is it! I know I'm going to get my release date set this time. Things are happening fast for me now. I've been here three years and all of a sudden here in a week everything is falling into place. I go to the Parole Board next month, and this morning I got a ducat for 11:15 to see Murray about doing my Board report.

Murray's office looks just the same, and so does he. That's why it's difficult to figure what the change is. He hasn't said anything more to me in the unit than he ever did, and he still gives me those left-handed questions, but something's changed. He doesn't seem so disapproving of me now. I guess that's the difference. He has to clean it up for himself that I'm somehow different, or changed, so he can let me out with a clear conscience.

When I walk into his office and hand him my ducat, he almost smiles.

"You wanted to see me?" I ask.

"Yes, Jimmy, come on in. I have to do your Board report."

"O.K."

"I see you only had the one disciplinary, two years ago. The Board will be impressed with that; they don't like troublemakers."

It's just like I thought; he's going to let me out, and he's trying to clean it up.

Yeah, he's going to let me out all right. I wonder what he'd say if I told him that? He'd probably give me some crap about "I don't really set your time, you do." Or else he'd say, "The Board sets your time; all I do is to write your report." Yeah, that's a laugh! *I set my time!* If I set my time I'd have been out three years ago. But that other con they give is even funnier. *The Board sets your time!* There are twenty-four thousand convicts in this state and the Board has to see them all once a year. It's really ridiculous that they expect anyone to believe the Board sets your time. All they do is tell you when you've got enough time in. It's Murray and hoosiers like him who really set the con's time. They're the ones who tell the Board what to do by writing these Board reports and saying whether you've been a good boy or a bad boy. With this

nothing, second-degree burglary beef, if I'd been a good
boy I'd have been out of here in two-and-a-half. But because I'm not a snitch and won't play their goofy games, I
knew when I came here I'd do three-and-a-half. Besides,
that's how much the Board makes a two-time loser do on a
burglary.

This indeterminate, one-to-fifteen year sentencing is a big
joke. It's still the same old thing—like flat time in the old
days—only with a new name. I'm doing as much time today
on the same beef as I would have done before they started
this indeterminate sentencing bullshit.

"You've been a hall porter," Murray says, "for two
years; that may not be too good for the Board. That's not
much of a job, especially if you come before Mr. Hinsley.
He used to be a counselor at this institution. Did you know
that?"

Did I know that? The only thing Murray forgot to
mention was that when he was here he was the biggest
prick that ever came down the pike.

"Yeah, I've heard."

"There's not too much we can do to minimize that,"
Murray goes on. "You can't look too good as a hall porter.
How come you didn't keep on with the welding when you
first came here?"

"I already have a trade. I'm a bartender."

Murray leafs through my jacket. He pauses for a minute,
writing notes to himself. "What about church? Do you go
to church?"

"No."

Man, he's really rushing me through. This is the sixth
Board report I've had done on me and the questions are
always the same; only most of the time the counselor takes
a little time and pains. He at least tries to make his job

look good. I guess Murray knows all he wants to know about me.

"Have you heard from your wife since the divorce?"

"Not directly, but I heard from other people she's doing all right."

She's doing all right, all right! But that broad won't be doing so good when I get out there!

"Do you think there's a chance of a reconciliation? This is probably one of the questions the Board will ask you."

Reconciliation! I'm going to reconcile her with a right hook!

"No chance."

"Well, I guess all we have to do now is explore a bit of the things you've learned about yourself since you've been here. We have to give the Board something to release you on, if that's their intention."

This is another part of the formality. I know what to say because I know what he wants to hear.

"I've learned a lot about myself," I answer. "I've gotten a lot of insight."

Murray looks a little pained, or tired, I'm not sure which.

"Listen," he says, "I think I know what you mean by that, but if you say that to the Board . . . if you say that to Mr. Hinsley, he's going to ask you what you mean."

"I think it's the divorce that really changed me—that really made me stop and think."

At that response, he gives me one of his long, groping looks, half-turns, looks out of the window, and bites at his lip. Then he turns back, reaches for my ducat, glances at his watch, notes the time and signs it, and hands it back to me. "O.K., Jimmy, we'll see you at the Board."

He is through with me.

I wonder if he's as glad to be through with me as I am to be finished with him!

Six Months Later:

That goddamned Tommy. He'd waited 'til the day before I went home to put the lug on me. He'd known that I was going home for the past six months, ever since I got my date at the Board. But he'd waited 'til now to strap his latest effort on me to get some junk.

This morning at breakfast he started off with "Say, Jimmy, I know how careful you try to be. But I'm going to ask you to do me a favor. You don't have to do it, you know, and I won't think nothing about it if you don't. But it sure would be nice if you sent back a little stuff for the fellows."

He knew I could hardly refuse. We'd been having breakfast together every morning for the past three-and-a-half years. Besides, we'd known each other on the streets. And he also knew that if I said I'd do it he'd get his junk.

I don't know how long he'd been planning it, but he sure had it laid out. Down to the finest detail. He had an absolutely foolproof master plan worked out. Because he knew I'd be short of dough when I first hit the streets, he had scrounged around and collected fifty bucks from the guys he knew I wouldn't mind sending a little stuff to. He had the bread and the route for the stuff back in. He even had a connection for me to look up when I hit the streets. But the best thing of all was that he had it all worked out how it was to come back. It was a work of art.

I was to buy two shaving brushes, the plastic, hollow kind, exactly alike. I was to knock the bottom off of one and the top off of the other until I had a whole, undamaged one. I was to take the stuff, put it in the handle in such a way that it wouldn't rattle; get some plastic cement and glue it up again; emery it off; and then send it to him like it was from his brother, who was on his mailing list.

But even better than all that, he already had it fixed with the con who works in the mail room to swing with it when it came. That way there would be a better chance than if the bull accidently stumbled on it. So he could alert the mail room con that it was coming, I was to send a postcard over his brother's name the day before I mailed the package, just saying that everything's fine and be seeing you soon.

Tommy was just too much! Before I even got out of this damn penitentiary he already had me taking chances on a ten-year beef with Uncle Sam. I knew they sort of frowned on sending heroin through the mails into the penitentiary.

*   *   *

But anyway, for now I'm getting out of this damn place. Everything held up. My shuck job outside, the phony one my dad arranged for me. All I have to do is give the guy a hundred dollars a week cash, and he'll give me a check for sixty-five, so I'll have a weekly payroll stub. If the parole agent or anyone else comes around asking for me, the guy will say I'm out on a delivery and that he will have me contact him as soon as I get back. In the meantime, he'll phone me to tell me that somebody's looking for me. They have a rule here that you have to have a place of employment while you're on parole, that you have to have a job before you can get out of prison. But they do so little checking that they don't know whether it's a real job or not. They're so easy to beat it's pitiful.

But today's my day! That means I'll be in action to-morrow! I know just what I'm going to do. The same thing I've done every time I've gotten out of any kind of jail. Tomorrow I'll start boosting 'til I get myself a good ward-robe. That ought to take three or four days. From there I'll be on the scene making the spots and trying to nail myself a broad. As soon as I do that I'll be in good shape. That ought to take a week. As soon as the broad starts bringing home that money every night, I'll make myself a down payment on a Caddy, and from there on it's all gravy.

They've let me go back home to my dad, so that means I'll have protection at the pad. My dad wouldn't tell a bull nothing if his life depended on it. I'll keep a few clothes at his house, as though I lived there. If anybody comes look-ing for me my dad'll just say that I've gone somewhere, but that I'll be right back; then, he too, will get in touch with me and let me know.

All the fellows that I have been tight with here in the joint managed to get stall ducats, like to the Chaplain's Office, or some other place that you don't really have to be, and came down to see me off. Tommy, Huey, Buddy, and Fat Paul were all hanging around laughing and scratch-ing and telling me, "Man, it was nothing but a cakewalk," referring to the three and a half years, and saying, "I got mine in, damn near now, so you'd better not stumble out there on those streets, 'cause I'll be right on your heels."

While we're waiting around 'til 8:15, when I'm scheduled to go down to the dress-out room, and put on that sack-cloth they give you to get out of here, I go into my cell to insert the half-hundred that Tommy gave me to buy the junk. They all stand around on the tier in front of my door and keep point for me while I put a little Vaseline hair tonic on the finger of a rubber glove, the kind they use in the kitchen to wash the hot trays with, and roll up the fifty dollars. I don't know how they managed to have so many one-dollar bills, because it makes such a great big roll, I can hardly handle it. Anyway, I grunt and insert the whole schmeer up my rectum. I didn't know a half-hundred would be so big!

I have already given all my stuff away to friends; my cell looks bleak and stark, and no longer like my home for the past three and a half years. In fact, it looks alien and strange to me because I am already mentally out of here and on my way to newer and bigger things! I'm really lost in here because now I don't belong.

The boys walk me up the long corridor toward the dress-out room and are hurrahing me all the way.

Tommy says, "Man, what are you walking like that for? You look like you're pigeon-toed. What's the matter, is something hurting the brunser?"

Everybody thinks that's very funny. But it isn't that funny to me because it does feel like I have a red-hot poker up my ass. Everything is fun and games, and the world is just a big ball. So what we don't do today, we'll do tomorrow, and if that turns out badly then there's always another day. If I get nailed with that half-hundred up my keester on the way out of here, then it'll cost me six months, and after that I'm right back where I started from, only six months later, and it ain't no big thing. Because I can outwait anybody. I got everything going for me. Everybody else is a sucker and my candy to take.

I'm going to kill them out there! All that good money from bad women or bad money from good women, it don't make no difference. I'm going to rip-and-tear and have a ball. I'm going to shoot junk, pimp whores, and tear holes in business roofs and live life the way it was meant to be lived. The world's mine and I'm going to kill them dead.

When we get to the big grill gate at the end of the corridor where I go on alone, the fellows all shake my hand and say things like, "We'll be hearing big things from you, Jimmy," and "Knock 'em dead, man, you've got everything going for you."

I shove my I.D. card and ducat through the barred grill gate to the bull; he flips the switch and the grill gate slides open. I am the only one leaving this morning, and my clothes are neatly hung on a hanger in the dress-out room. Sergeant Chavez goes in with me to shake me down and watch me dress. After I've taken off all my clothes, he runs his fingers through my hair to make sure I have nothing there, looks under my arms and feels in my armpits, has me lift my scrotum to see that nothing is taped there, has me bend over and spread the cheeks so that he can determine that I have nothing there (though he'll have to run his finger up there to find out!), looks at the bottoms of my feet and between my toes to make sure nothing is there, and then tells me to get dressed.

Putting on outside clothes, even though of this variety, really makes me feel good after three and a half years of blue denims. All I can think of is, "Yeah, man, I'm going to kill them dead. The whole world is my oyster and it's a great big fat one!"

After I've dressed, Sergeant Chavez escorts me through the two more grilled gates out back to the industrial area where the main gate is. While we are walking, I see Murray coming toward us; he is going to work. I look the other way, out over the industrial area, so I won't have to say anything.

When we approach the main gate, old Sergeant Buehler starts his usual and traditional patter.

"What have we got here?" he says. "What did the Board do, make another mistake? Are we going to let this one out, too? It gets worse here every day!"

I ignore the asshole, even if he is a pretty good bull; he's been around for twenty years and he knows cons. But Sergeant Chavez answers, "Yes, here's another one for you, Charlie."

Old Buehler throws the main switch and the grill gate starts sliding back. The world is just three feet from me now. When I walk by, Buehler gives out with his classic parting shot, "We'll save your bunk for you, Dunn, you'll be needing it."

I don't even look back. I am on my way. This is it. My steps get faster and faster because I just want to be away from this goddamn place. Everything I want in the world is right out there before me now. I have it, I have it in my grasp, and I am going to kill them dead!

Chapter 11

Implications

A Game with No Winners

LaMAR T. EMPEY:

The introduction to this book on the prison game painted a dismal picture. The actual game, as played by Dunn, Murray, and the other players did little to alter that picture. However, before we consider its implications, let us consider the literature on prisons. It will help to pinpoint the crucial issues.

On one hand, there is a great deal of conjecture, and some evidence, that an integrated inmate system arises in prison in response to the debasing effects of captivity (Sykes, 1958; Sykes and Messinger, 1960; McCorkle and

Korn, 1954). An inmate organization develops which is epitomized by a prison code whose function is resistance to formal authority and the maintenance of self-dignity (Clemmer, 1940; Schrag, 1954; Sykes, 1958; Sykes and Messinger, 1960; Wheeler, 1961; Schrag, 1961; and Garabedian, 1963). The basic notion is that inmate organization is primarily a product of the degrading effects of institutional life, a result of the character of correctional organizations (Goffman, 1961).

On the other hand, the evidence in favor of this notion is not totally compelling (Tittle, 1969). Several investigations have noted that inmate organization is by no means completely successful in mitigating the devastating effects of social rejection and captivity. Prison life is characterized by considerable individualism and personal isolation (Clemmer, 1940; Morris and Morris, 1963; Glaser, 1964). Further, some inmates are unwilling to accept the standards of the inmate code and remain essentially prosocial, i.e., "Square Johns" (Schrag, 1961) or legitimately oriented inmates (Irwin and Cressey, 1964).

To complicate this matter further, besides the likelihood that the inmate organization is not totally unified, the same might be said of formal authority. The notion of a monolithic official structure is a myth (Schrag, 1961). Officials in any prison usually possess different ideologies and are fragmented into competing subsystems by virtue of their different roles. The most notable fracture exists between treatment and custody people. But even within these groups, there are competing, vested interests. Clinical personnel, diagnosticians, and counselors are often at odds with educational and vocational people. They simply do not agree with respect to basic goals and methods. The official organization may be as fragmented as the inmate organization.

The discussion by Dunn and Murray did little to dispel the basic themes just described. However, it did suggest some important, and often subtle, variations which should be taken into account.

Overall Prison Organization

The descriptions by Dunn and Murray strongly suggest that inmate and overall prison organizations can scarcely be understood one without the other. That is, in contrast to the notion that inmate and official organizations should be seen mainly in terms of their opposition to each other, it might be wise to focus upon the *symbiotic* character of their relationship as well. Although they are dissimilar, they are also highly interdependent. As two subsystems within the same overall structure, each helps to dictate the character of the other. The reason for their symbiosis is inherent in the nature of the general framework that is imposed upon them. Officials as well as inmates are captives of a societal legacy which still places confidence in the utility of confinement, both as a corrective device and as a means of protecting society. Many progressive correctional people, recognizing the limitations of this legacy, have attempted to introduce change by working *within* the prison, i.e., to utilize the principle of operant conditioning as a means of educating and training offenders (Cohen, 1968; McKee, 1964), to establish careers in corrections for former offenders (Grant and Grant, 1967), or to use various forms of the therapeutic community (Jones, 1953; Studt, et al., 1968). But one must be cautious about the extent to which the adoption of new treatment methods in a total institution can successfully eliminate the negative effects of the division of staff and offenders into mutually exclusive superordinate and subordinate castes. Even though their announced objectives, and some of their practices, are different from sheer custody, many of the same problems remain.

The reason lies in the tendency for treatment, like punishment philosophies, to concentrate upon the problems of the individual at the expense of considering organizational and power arrangements. The problems of change have rarely been conceived in structural terms. As a consequence, new methods have never seriously come to grips with the basic organizational question: can resocialization occur in a caste system?

If there is much validity to the problems which Dunn and Murray describe, then the answer may be "no." So long as the overall prison structure remains caste-like, then it would not seem likely that most people could take its resocialization function seriously. The notion of having inmates and officials adopt and share the same set of values and activities is a logical contradiction. If it does nothing else, the system is effective in keeping them apart. Consider an analogy.

The nature of this kind of a system was illustrated by a popular movie of the mid-1960s, *The Sand Pebbles* (compare Empey, 1968). The movie was the story of an American gunboat in China during the turbulent 1920s. The crew of the *Sand Pebbles* had worked out an interesting, informal arrangement by which they got their work done. Virtually every officer and sailor on that ship had a Chinese coolie who was his counterpart on the bridge, on the deck, in the galley, and in the engine room. It was this informal crew, many of whom could not even speak English, who kept the ship running. Yet, insofar as the United States Navy was officially concerned, the Chinese members of the crew did not even exist. If you looked at the Table of Organization for the ship, you could not see one of them represented.

The point is that the *Sand Pebbles* was much like a traditional prison or reform school. It was a caste system in which the upper caste—the crew—was concerned with the job performance of the lower caste—the Chinese—primarily in terms of its ability to contribute to the running of a smooth ship. It is true that coolie leaders were permitted, indeed expected, to exercise considerable power and controls over *other* coolies. But no thought was ever given to the possibility that the Chinese should share in decision-making with the crew, that the two castes should interact socially with each other, or that the shipboard experience could ever be used as a means for preparing the Chinese for a career in the Navy. Indeed, even in their wildest fantasies, it is unlikely that the members of either caste, most of all the American crew, ever entertained that notion. Thus, while there was some pay-off for the Chinese crew—primarily in terms of physical necessities and creature comforts—that pay-off was an integral part of their membership in the lower caste and did not extend beyond it; that is, the caste system was extended into the larger society. In fact, the reader may recall that one young coolie was brutally murdered by other Chinese because he had worked on the ship. Rather than serving to integrate him in the larger society, his work proved to be a source of stigma. In fact, his membership in the crew placed him in a kind of no-man's-land where he was accepted neither by the American upper caste as one of them, nor by his countrymen as one of them.

The parallel between this and the predicament of an incarcerated delinquent is so obvious as to need little elaboration. The offender is stigmatized by society, and he is certainly not accepted by the institutional staff as one of them. Consequently, the only place he has to turn for a sense of identity and a definition of purpose is the inmate caste. Theoretically, at least, this is precisely what we do not want to happen; we would like the offender to identify with prosocial points of view and to take on conformist characteristics which will enable him to function effectively as a noncriminal. Given the nature of correctional caste systems, however, the only roles open for the offender are roles associated with the inmate caste. A fundamental question for contemporary corrections, therefore, is what the prospects are for changing the traditional caste systems found in correctional organizations.

A resolution of this issue will require attention to specific issues relative to the two major castes, and to the subgroups within them. Consider Dunn, and people like him. To what extent could one expect to deal with him outside of a rigid system? To what extent does his commitment to crime make him a serious threat to the community? Is a prison the only alternative for him?

Good will alone cannot provide the answers to these questions. One of the glaring inadequacies in our present body of knowledge is information upon which to base offender typologies and logically derived intervention strategies. In addition to the need to alter the prison caste system, we need information by which we can determine the extent to which the criminal orientations of some offenders contribute to the maintenance of that system and information on the interactional processes which occur when these tendencies are combined with prison structure.

There are two dimensions to this issue which must be considered. First, given the symbiotic character of official and inmate systems, there are grounds for arguing that habitual criminals, no less than officials, would resist change in the system. Paradoxically, the inmate system probably continues to operate because it aids in the control function of the prison. An accommodation between authorities and inmates evolves in which considerable power is exercised by inmate leaders. Rackets, exploitation, and even violence, when confined to offenders, remain hidden so long as inmate leaders are successful in preventing the eruption of overt conflict between inmate and official systems. This accommodation encourages the status quo— keeping things as they are. The pay-off for the official organization is the maintenance of order. The pay-off for the criminally-oriented inmate is that he is spared, not only the necessity of having to change, but the threat of losing considerable power to his captors. Thus, the relationship between officials and criminally-oriented, inmate leaders is symbiotic. Both help to perpetuate existing arrangements.

A second source of cohesion among inmates was implied in Dunn's description of some of the more degrading and brutal aspects of prison life. "Despite all the time I have spent in prison," he once said, "it is a terrifying place to me, it is hopeless. Can you imagine five thousand guys all jammed into one little yard, and half of them spooky?" His remarks suggest another function performed by the inmate system. It seems likely that some of the apparent solidarity among those in the inmate caste may be more of a defensive and protective device than an organizational mechanism in pursuit of some higher objective. The inmate system not only defines ways of relating to the official caste but provides a means of social control within the inmate caste. For the prison-wise inmate, especially, it helps him to engage in a kind of overt conformity to official rules, so as to keep his record unsullied by any incident, while maintaining, at the same time, a degree of power within the system. He is able to keep up an outward appearance of good behavior without having to change.

One can only imagine the difficult position in which this places the legitimately oriented inmate. He is indeed isolated, forced to walk a fine line between the pressures of official and inmate systems. Even Dunn, with all his experience, expresses fear for his own safety, or the possibility that he will be drawn into some activity which can be harmful to him. This fear is illustrated either by his contempt for those "hoosiers" who rush to the dispensary with feigned illness in order to obtain a new cough syrup which has codeine in it, by his attempts to avoid becoming involved in the dealings of a friend in smuggled "junk," or by his efforts to prevent Murray and the group from discussing an inmate stabbing. Furthermore, these same incidents also illustrate the extent to which Murray and Small, and people like them, are also isolated by the system. It is apparent that they can do little so long as they are caught in the conflicting machinations of official and inmate power structures. They either give up, as Small did, or leave the system, as Murray did.

Thus, if one wished to sort out the complex web of personal and organizational characteristics that are found in a prison, he would need: (1) better classifications of inmates by which to determine the degree of criminal or legitimate orientations they bring to the prison; (2) more complete knowledge of the extent to which the inmate system serves as a mechanism for social control among inmates and how different types of inmates relate to it; and (3) greater information on the subtle and symbiotic relationships which seem to exist between inmate and official castes. Further, one would need a better understanding of the subsystems within the official caste, as well, and of the extent to which people like Murray or Small, as well as individual inmates, were isolated by virtue of the roles they play. Such information might then go a long way toward answering the basic question raised earlier, namely, the extent to which total institutions can be expected to deal effectively with the problems of rehabilitation and change.

Second, we need to know whether a treatment, as contrasted to a punitive, orientation among staff can be expected to alter basic organizational problems. Despite the fact that a treatment orientation and professional training are supposed to be antidotes to the punitive practices of the past, there is reason to question that assumption. Given the symbiotic character of the relationship between staff and offenders, especially when it occurs in a setting of total confinement, pressures remain which make difficult the derivation of new and productive roles for offenders. The reason is that the status of the professional, his helping role, his very place in the scheme of things, depends heavily upon the offender remaining in a subordinate role to him.

The treatment idea has its roots in a medical model. Thus, even if the criminal is defined as "sick" rather than "wicked," the social consequences of that definition are much the same, especially if he is removed from the community and isolated for treatment. The label of undesirability is retained, and the community's negative perception of the offender is retained. As a result, it is difficult for the offender to ever conceive of himself as anything other than "criminal" or "inmate." Little or no effort has been made to develop means by which an offender might be moved step-by-step into new and legitimate roles—roles which would bring new rewards, decrease stigma, and decrease social distance between staff and inmate groups. What is needed, it would seem, is some reconceptualization of both offender and staff roles in social and organizational terms. The socialization and induction of offenders into legitimate roles is something far different and more complex than the mere alteration of something within *him*.

What is implied, of course, is a set of problems which the prison seems ill-equipped to address, namely, the effective linkage of offenders with ordinary institutions and practices in the community. The community, like the prison, requires realteration of many of its institutional deficiencies and role prescriptions. No less than in the prison, there are obstructions in the community which block a change in the social roles of those offenders who are interested in change. Thus, a reasonable conclusion might be that, while the grounds are not adequate for arguing that the prison as a protective device for the community can yet be eliminated, present conditions leave little room for believing that it is an effective rehabilitative device. It is difficult to be anything but pessimistic.

Given the problems which have already been discussed, it seems clear that inmates who remain free of crime after release from prison may do so more in spite of their experience rather than because ot it, or because punishment of this type works for some people. The possible pains of reinvolvement are simply too much for them to ever risk again. The residue of remaining problems, however, is tremendous.

Apropos of these problems, one of the most compelling and distressing aspects of the story by Dunn and Murray has to do with the unwritten and informal prison games which people play with each other. The most obvious game, of course, is between staff and inmates. Staff members are obviously aware of the manipulations and deceit of people like Dunn. They know what he is trying to do and why he is trying to do it. But they are prisoners in their own system. Because of the official rules by which they operate, and in the absence of productive work and other activities for him, they have no mechanisms by which they can document his deceit or provide him with alternatives for it. So long as he conforms to their formal demands, they are trapped.

In a most telling commentary, both Dunn and Murray describe the prison as a smothering mother. Everything is supplied for the inmate (witness Dunn's mouthful of gold fillings, all provided by a benificent state); he is even told when to get up in the morning and when to go to bed. Thus, in the absence of means by which to demand that he exercise any responsibility, there are no means by which to correct or penalize him when he does not. In such a setting, therefore, manipulation and overt conformity, not learning and a change in behavior, is the name of the game.

The same sorts of games occur within the inmate and official systems as well. No one can escape. The various actors in the official system, for example—the custody, work, and treatment people—do not really solve their differences; they only accommodate each other. They stay in operation by a continual series of tradeoffs. Chuvalo gives in on one point in return for concessions by Murray on another—all unspoken, but very real nonetheless. Thus, among officials, as well as among inmates, it will be the most skillful manipulator who most often gets what he wants. And if daily manipulation, rather than a straightforward attack on problems is evidence of human corruption, then everyone is corrupted.

To the reader, indeed to the various actors, the moves in these prison games are evidence of their debasing effect. One of the most fascinating aspects of Dunn's and Murray's commentaries was that, while the motives and actions of each of the participants was patently clear to the other, each retained the fantasy that his actions alone were inscrutable, that he was fooling the other. What was suggested, therefore, was not only self-delusion but a kind of game in which there really were no winners.

Evidence of corruption even extended to the measures taken to get Dunn released from prison. Dunn knew that he had not changed, but was more than willing to carry out a charade with Murray in order to get an acceptable statement prepared for the Parole Board. It was as though an honest approach would be worse than the deceit because Murray also knew that Dunn had not changed and was lying to him, but he felt constrained to play his part. Given the hopelessness of the situation, he knew that he had to fabricate a statement that would appeal to the prejudices of the Parole Board. Even they were contributors to the charade. It should come as no surprise, then, to learn that, as Dunn left the prison, he did so with a contraband roll of fifty one-dollar bills inserted painfully into his rectum. He had agreed to use the money to buy dope for his friends and to smuggle it illegally back into the prison.

Postscript

What Happened to Jimmy Dunn?

LaMAR T. EMPEY:

The seemingly irrevocable course of Dunn's life did not turn when he left the prison. He was soon involved again in prostitution, armed robbery, burglary, and narcotics usage and sale. It was the latter which led very quickly to another conviction and confinement for five years in a federal prison. Again, the experience was not helpful. Within a few months after his release from this term, he was rearrested and sent to a special institution for addicts. This time, however, something occurred which Jimmy recalls as having "shook him up."

Officials in the new institution refused to accept Dunn and returned him to court. They felt that his history of violence and habitual criminality was too much for them to control, especially since they were charged with helping addicts on civil as well as criminal commitments. The court, however, would not honor this rejection and reordered the same placement. Perhaps, surprisingly, this experience had an impact on Dunn—being rejected even by a correctional facility—and caused him to consider the seriousness of his predicament. It seemed to dawn on him that his life was going down the drain, at least if "time on the streets" meant anything. Although he was now thirty, his longest period of freedom from confinement since age fourteen had been six and one-half months. His thinking seemed to parallel that of many other offenders who, when asked why they stopped using dope and committing crimes, report that they "just got tired." The ceaseless hassle of maintaining a habit became too much for them. At any rate, Dunn seemed to take his new placement more seriously and to become more heavily committed to a process of change. As evidence of this commitment, Dunn's life did make an abrupt turn after two more years of confinement. And, surprisingly, it was his old "friend" Murray who helped him to make that turn.

When Dunn was released he contacted Murray who, by now, had left the prison system and was working in the community. He sought help from Murray for two reasons: he wanted a job; and he had been released from the institution with but twenty dollars from the state and bus fare to the city. Murray not only welcomed Dunn and put him up for a few days, but helped him get a job. Murray was aware of a new experimental program for delinquents which was just beginning and arranged for Dunn to be hired as an interviewer and research assistant on the project.

Even the mere employment of Dunn on such a project, however, had all kinds of implications. On one hand, despite the lack of experience with the formal aspects of a research role, Dunn possessed many attributes which were in his favor: he was personable, neat, and articulate (anyone seeing him would think he was a bright, young businessman), and his personal knowledge of delinquency provided him with a background for approaching, communicating with, and interviewing other delinquents. On the other hand, Dunn had very little formal education—he had never gone beyond the ninth grade. Furthermore, except for his short, unsuccessful service in the Merchant Marines, *he had never before held a regular job*, something that is certainly uncommon in a person thirty-two years of age. Thus, the question as to whether he could successfully hold a job was a serious one, especially since he would be working with academic types with whom he had had little or no experience. But Dunn was gifted, and could interact effectively, either in social or work situations. These talents, plus his intellectual capacities, resulted in his doing remarkably well on the job. It was not long, therefore, before he was given increased responsibility, based not only upon his interpersonal skills, but productivity and unusually hard work. He became a valuable member of the staff. Simultaneously, he successfully completed a college entrance exam and entered a city college. Over a two-year period, he successfully met the responsibilities of his full-time job, carried a full load in college, where he maintained a B+ average, and successfully complied with all the requirements of parole, including nalline testing for narcotics usage which made him ill each time he tested.

Near the end of the two-year period, he met and married an attractive, professional woman. Dunn's enthusiasm for college work so infected his wife that she too returned to the university to work for a graduate degree. His aspiration had now become that of obtaining a Ph.D., and she joined in. During the next year, they acquired all of the trappings of a successful middle-class couple: an attractive apartment, cars, mutual friends, and even a savings account.

Meanwhile, Dunn's change was so striking to correctional people, familiar with the high failure rate among former addicts, that he was given special attention by them when speaking on occasion to various offender and correctional groups, to college classes, and elsewhere. Thus, he not only completed three years of parole supervision successfully, but did so in a way that brought him special recognition. Then began his descent from the summit.

Without going into all of the details of the descent, Dunn's performance on the job and in the university began to deteriorate. For a long time it was difficult for his employers and friends to pinpoint the reasons for an increasing number of difficulties. What had happened, of course, was that Dunn had returned to narcotics and was trying to live a double life. With little or no difficulty, he had reestablished relationships with some of his criminal friends who apparently welcomed him back with no censure whatsoever—in fact, Dunn's return simply confirmed their cynical belief that a person who is both a heroin user and an habitual offender can never really change. Only Dunn's wife knew what was going on, and she was so loyal and committed to helping him that she covered up for him.

During the second year of the decline, Dunn's difficulties could no longer remain hidden. His absences from work, his lack of productivity, and his excessive spending resulted in several painful sessions with his employers, and a bed of pain for his wife. Dunn seemed to try on several occasions to reverse the trend, but it was difficult to tell whether his efforts were serious or merely manipulative. His basic talents and likableness were so obvious, on one hand, and he had spent so many years conning citizens, counselors, and institutional personnel, on the other, that he could make almost anyone believe in him. It was, and still is, difficult to tell just how much of Dunn is a thoroughgoing con man and how much is a fundamentally attractive and talented man who may be capable of surmounting a life of familial and social rejection. Most likely, he is an undetermined admixture of both.

At the time of this writing, five years after his last release from prison, he has broken all of his new ties—left his job, dropped out of the university, a few units short of graduation, separated from his wife, leaving her with thousands of dollars of debts, and, following an almost classic pattern of reversion, returned to live with his father in a second-rate hotel apartment. What led to this state of affairs? How did it come about?

First, the significance of Dunn's achievements during five years of freedom should not be overlooked. Given his background, they are little short of miraculous. Consider the changes he tried to make.

Without ever having enjoyed the security of a home, a formal education, and work experience, moving from a life on the streets and in institutions, knowing only pimps, prostitutes, and criminals for friends, and having become accustomed to the immediate gratifications of heroin, he tried in a few short years to adopt a life style which was just the opposite—to become educated, to work, to marry, to associate with people whose backgrounds were alien to him, and, most of all, to become a seeker of deferred, not short-range, gratifications. The magnitude of such a change, both personal and social, is incredible. Indeed, does not Dunn's dilemma speak to the larger problem of offender rehabilitation? Who among us could make the changes he attempted and be successful?

Dunn himself recognized the difficulty of the task only in part. In a recent conversation, we tried to analyze what had happened. At first, he was inclined to blame himself. With his chin quivering, he said, "I destroyed everything, my marriage, my hopes for graduate study, and my relationships with those who trusted me. I destroyed everything."

It was possible, of course, that he was merely saying the things he thought I wanted to hear, but I do not believe so. He was in town for only a few minutes and had little to gain from me.

"I ran away again," he said, "and what worries me is that I didn't recognize the danger signals. I had the world by the tail, and then I went out and fixed. Why?

"Do you know that I have been like a madman the past eighteen months? I have lived in my car, running frantically from one place to another, stealing things, trying to scrape enough together to make a connection. I've been so frantic I've even scared the hell out of my suppliers.

"Do you know that during the same time I've tried to 'kick' six times, cold turkey? Last summer I spent my vacation in a tent, in the mountains, trying to kick. My poor wife just sat by trying to keep me warm—trying to help in some way."

Then he switched to his pseudonym, Dunn, to describe himself. "The only thing I can see in Dunn is his rigidity. He does well on the surface but he just doesn't hold up. Deeply, he destroys everything time and time again. He has no flexibility."

I asked him to explain what he meant by "flexibility," and it was this question which led to a more complex set of problems—problems for which no amount of personal guilt on Dunn's part could be totally responsible. His answer introduced the whole range of social as well as psychological issues which must be considered in any analysis of his (or anyone's) behavior.

"Well," said Dunn, "I worked for a group of people whom I sincerely believe were trying to be my friends. Nevertheless, I could never get rid of a nagging, little doubt in the back of my mind. I always felt out of place. In fact, I have never been flexible enough to get over my sense of inadequacy.

"When I was still a kid I had a difficult time switching from being a 'hard guy' in the street gang to a cool professional. It was the second most difficult change I have ever tried to make. The most difficult change was this last one. It was even harder to play the middle-class role. I have never experienced a complete sense of belonging anywhere."

Even though he tended to blame himself, Dunn was only partially correct. What he was experiencing were the self-doubts of marginal men everywhere, only in his case the problems, if anything, were more difficult. He did not really comprehend the implications of what he had attempted, that of moving from the world of the streets and state institutions, to the world of middle-class academia. It was not merely that he had to adjust to different people and the norms by which they live, but a world that may be far more impersonal and instrumentally-oriented than the one he had left. The world of the intellectual or academic, for example, can be a very lonely world when judged by many standards.

In fact, it is worth pausing to note the dilemma which Dunn's problems created for his associates at work, as well as for himself. Hypothetically, since they were studying delinquent behavior, they should have had some answers for him. Ironically, however, they were captives of their own professional norms in somewhat the same way prison officials were captives of their system. In any professional group, there is a reluctance to pry into the lives of one's peers, especially to place stringent limits upon them the way a correctional agency or parole officer might do. This reluctance is based, not just upon a set of impersonal relations alone, but upon respect for one's associates as well. Therefore, even when danger signals appeared, Dunn's friends at work found themselves bound by these professional norms. While they did counsel him, did eventually ask difficult questions, and did attempt to provide supports, they were reluctant to take up a kind of police action. They were constrained to accept his statements at face value, even when they suspected the worst. Thus, while Dunn might have been helped had greater demands been placed upon him, the nature of his work situation seemed to preclude it.

Paradoxically, Dunn's comments suggest the possibility that had an exception been made in his case, it might have helped him. "There were times," he said, "when I felt that all that was important were my work skills. I felt like a cog in a machine. So much of what I was doing I had to do alone—reviewing literature, analyzing data, and so on. It was so impersonal that I felt I was important more for what I did, than what I was. A person has to be a self-contained atom to survive in that world. He operates most of the time in a private little cell, and the rewards he gets from his work are so far out *there*, so long in coming. Finally, there is so much one has to tend to: work, grades, wife, money, and possessions. It just got too much for me. I wanted out, and I got out.

"By contrast, the world of the hype has only one purpose—the next fix. If I don't have the 'stuff' today, and my friend does, we share it until it's gone. Then when I have some, I'll share it with him. Life is so simple."

In growing nostalgia over his former life, Dunn failed to recognize the contradictory themes that had characterized his few short statements. Only a few moments before he had described himself as having "destroyed everything," as having failed once more to leave a "frantic" and "terrifying" life. Now he was describing that life as simple and rewarding.

Despite these contradictions, it did not seem that Dunn merely lacked insight or was trying to be deceitful. Instead, his remarks probably provide an accurate picture of the dilemma which confronted him. *He was profoundly ambivalent.* His recent experiences in the world of convention, like those in the criminal world, had been both good and bad, both pleasant and unpleasant. An ambivalent state of affairs, however, was not limited to Dunn. His dilemma was by no means unique. It was reflective instead of the larger human condition in which few of the major choices one must make in life are without their negative as well as positive consequences. Thus, there are some lessons inherent in his plight which have implications for society, in general, and for correctional people in particular.

While it was true that Dunn had not made the final choice as to what course he would follow, at least his experience in the conventional world had provided him with an alternative. The same could not be said, however, of the prison. There are few ways there by which the offender, especially a serious one like Dunn, can be confronted with even the possibility of conventional success. Thus he is not even brought to the position where he can assess the choice between conventionality and further criminality in a realistic way. At least it appears that he had been confronted with that choice. How it would turn out is another matter.

Second, Dunn's dilemma speaks to the naivete which is inherent in some of our humanistic and theoretical traditions; namely, if people in trouble, whether poor, of minority groups, or criminal, are merely provided with the *opportunity* to succeed, they will automatically do so. One lesson we can learn from Dunn, like those we have learned in the areas of poverty and civil rights, is that opportunity alone is not enough. In an overt sense, Dunn had numerous opportunities—a reasonably good job, an education, and a marriage—but they were not enough. Opportunity needs redefinition to include far more of the social and psychological changes that will be required if it is to have any meaning.

It would be nice to end this story on a happy note, but that is impossible. The outcome is still in doubt; Dunn is still struggling with the alternatives. Dunn, it will be recalled, has returned to live with his father. He said he sought out his father as a kind of refuge where, without the pressures he was experiencing, he could try to kick his habit and think things out.

On the positive side, it seemed as though he was treating his return to his father as a symbolic effort to reconstruct the family life he never had. He also reported that he intends to attend the college in his home town in order to complete the few courses he needs for his B.A. degree. Ironically, however, all of the old and deviant alternatives are there if he chooses them. "Wouldn't you know it," he said, "the day after I returned home I ran into one of my old friends and his broad. They live only two doors down the hall from my father's room. The guy is on stuff and she is working that street to support him."

Dunn's life is still balanced on a fulcrum.

References

REFERENCES

CLEMMER, D. (1940) The Prison Community. Boston: Christopher Publishing.

COHEN, H. (1968) "Educational therapy: the design of learning environments." Research in Psychotherapy 3: 21-53.

CRESSEY, D. (1968) "Administrative policy, staff and client opinions pertaining to the offender as a manpower resource in the administration of justice." Offenders as a Correctional Manpower Resource. Washington, D. C.: Joint Commission on Correctional Manpower and Training.

EMPEY, L. T. (1968) "Offender participation in the correctional process: general theoretical issues." In Offenders as a Correctional Manpower Resource. Washington, D. C.: Joint Commission on Correctional Manpower and Training.

GARABEDIAN, P. G. (1963) "Social roles and processes of socialization in the prison community." Social Problems 11 (Fall): 139-152.

GLASER, D. (1964) The Effectiveness of a Prison and Parole System. Indianapolis: Bobbs-Merrill.

GOFFMAN, E. (1961) "On the characteristics of total institutions: the inmate world." P. 15 in D. R. Cressey (ed.) The Prison. New York: Holt, Rinehart & Winston.

GRANT, J. D. and J. GRANT (1967) New Careers Development Project, Final Report. National Institute of Mental Health.

IRWIN, J. and D. R. CRESSEY (1964) "Thieves, convicts, and the inmate culture." P. 225 in H. S. Becker (ed.) The Other Side. New York: Free Press.

Joint Commission on Correctional Manpower and Training (1968)
    The Public Looks at Crime and Corrections. Washington, D. C.

JONES, M. (1953) The Therapeutic Community: A New Treatment
    Method in Psychiatry. New York: Basic Books.

McCORKLE L. W. and R. KORN (1954) "Resocialization within
    walls." Annals 293 (May).

McKEE, J. (1964) "The Draper experiment: a program learning
    project." In G. D. Ofiesh and W. C. Meierhenry (eds.) Trends in
    Programmed Instruction. Washington, D. C.: National Education
    Association.

MORRIS, T. and P. MORRIS (1963) Pentonville: A Sociological
    Study of an English Prison. London: Routledge & Kegan Paul.

SCHRAG, C. (1961) "Some foundations for a theory of correction."
    P. 309 in D. R. Cressey (ed.) The Prison. New York: Holt,
    Rinehart & Winston.
——— (1954) "Leadership among prison inmates." American Socio-
    logical Review 19 (February): 37-42.

SHAW, C. (1966) The Jack-Roller: A Delinquent Boy's Own Story.
    Chicago: Chicago University Press.

STUDT, E., S. L. MESSINGER, and T. P. WILSON [eds.] (1968)
    C-Unit: Search for Community in Prison. New York: Russell
    Sage Foundation.

SYKES, G. M. (1958) Society of Captives. Princeton: Princeton
    University Press.

SYKES, G. M. and S. L. MESSINGER (1960) "The inmate social
    system." Theoretical Studies in Social Organization of the
    Prison. Social Science Research Council Pamphlet No. 15
    (March): 5-19.

TITTLE, C. R. (1969) "Inmate organization: sex differentiation and the influence of criminal subcultures." American Sociological Review 34 (August): 492-504.

WHEELER, S. (1961) "Role conflict in correctional communities." The Prison. New York: Holt, Rinehart & Winston.

A Checklist of Sage Professional Journals

AMERICAN BEHAVIORAL SCIENTIST
Published bi-monthly. Each issue devoted to a significant topic or area of interdisciplinary research.

JOURNAL OF BLACK STUDIES
Published quarterly. Research and analytical discussion on significant social, political, economic questions related to persons of African descent.

CRIMINOLOGY: An Interdisciplinary Journal
Published quarterly. Research on crime, criminology and related social questions.

COMPARATIVE GROUP STUDIES
Published quarterly. Research and theory in all fields of small group study, including therapy groups.

COMPARATIVE POLITICAL STUDIES
Published quarterly. Theoretical and empirical research articles in cross-national comparative studies.

JOURNAL OF COMPARATIVE ADMINISTRATION
Published quarterly. Cross-national, interdisciplinary research on public organizations.

DESIGN METHODS GROUP NEWSLETTER
Published monthly. A compilation of research news, abstracts, etc., from architecture, civil engineering, city and regional planning and regional science.

EDUCATION AND URBAN SOCIETY
Published quarterly. Social research with implications for public policy.

ENVIRONMENT AND BEHAVIOR
   Published quarterly. Concerned with study, design and control of the physical environment and its interaction with human behavior.

LAW AND SOCIETY REVIEW
   Published quarterly. Studies of law as a social and political phenomenon and as an instrument of public policy.

SIMULATION AND GAMES
   Published quarterly. International journal of theory, design and research.

URBAN AFFAIRS QUARTERLY
   Published quarterly. International and interdisciplinary focus on all areas of urban research.

URBAN EDUCATION
   Published quarterly. Empirical and theoretical papers aimed at improving education in the city.

URBAN RESEARCH NEWS
   Published bi-weekly. Reports current developments in all areas of urban research.

URBAN STUDIES
   Published three times a year. International journal of urban and regional studies.

YOUTH AND SOCIETY
   Published quarterly. Research articles on social, psychological, political, and other problems and questions relating to youth in contemporary society.

For Subscription and Other Information Write To:
Dept. T, Sage Publications, 275 South Beverly Drive, Beverly Hills, Calif. 90212

A Selected List of Sage Publications

THE VOLUNTARY WORKER IN THE SOCIAL SERVICES
Geraldine Aves, et al.
224 pp.   1970

SIMULATION GAMES IN LEARNING
Sarane S. Boocock and E. O. Schild
320 pp.   1968

BEHAVIOR IN NEW ENVIRONMENTS:
Adaptation of Migrant Populations
Eugene B. Brody, ed.
480 pp.   1970

MORAL EDUCATION
Norman J. Bull
190 pp.   1970

MORAL JUDGEMENT FROM CHILDHOOD TO ADOLESCENCE
Norman J. Bull
316 pp.   1970

INFLUENCING THE YOUTH CULTURE:
A Study of Youth Organizations in Israel
Joseph W. Eaton in collaboration with Michael Chen
256 pp.   1970

URBAN POWER AND SOCIAL WELFARE:
Corporate Influence in an American City
Richard E. Edgar
224 pp.   1970

EDUCATING AN URBAN POPULATION
Marilyn Gittell, ed.
320 pp.   (cloth and paper)   1967

ANGRY ADOLESCENTS
Ronald Goldman
128 pp.   1969

THE METROPOLITAN COMMUNITY: Its People and Government
Amos H. Hawley and Basil G. Zimmer
160 pp. (cloth and paper) 1969

LEARNING THROUGH DISCUSSION:
Guide for Leaders and Members of Discussion Groups
Wm. Fawcett Hill
64 pp.   1969

SOCIOLOGICAL-SELF IMAGES: A Collective Portrait
Irving Louis Horowitz, ed.
256 pp. (cloth and paper) 1969

THE STATE OF THE UNIVERSITY: Authority and Change
Carlos E. Kruytbosch and Sheldon L. Messinger, eds.
384 pp. (cloth and paper) 1970

RIOTS AND REBELLION: Civil Violence in the Urban Community
Louis H. Masotti and Don R. Bowen, eds.
464 pp. (cloth and paper) 1968

THE COURT AND LOCAL LAW ENFORCEMENT:
The Impact of Miranda
Neal A. Milner
288 pp.   1970

CLIENTS COME LAST: Volunteers and Welfare Organizations
Esther Stanton
192 pp.   1970

THE PSYCHEDELIC EXPERIENCE: A Sociological Study
David W. Watts, Jr.
224 pp.   1970

SAGE PUBLICATIONS/275 S. Beverly Dr./Beverly Hills, Cal. 90212

URBAN AFFAIRS ANNUAL REVIEWS

This series of annual reference volumes provides critical analyses of significant topics relevant to the problems and prospects of urban life. Programs, policies, and current developments in a wide range of areas are covered. Each annual volume is published in the Spring. Write for further details.

Volume 1   1967
Urban Research and Policy Planning
Edited by **Leo F. Schnore** and **Henry Fagin**

Volume 2   1968
Power, Poverty, and Urban Policy
Edited by **Warner Bloomberg, Jr.** and **Henry J. Schmandt**

Volume 3   1969
The Quality of Urban Life
Edited by **Henry J. Schmandt** and **Warner Bloomberg, Jr.**

Volume 4   1970
Financing the Metropolis: Public Policy in Urban Economies
Edited by **John P. Crecine**

Volume 5   1971
Race and Cities
Edited by **Peter Orleans** and **William Russell Ellis**

SAGE PUBLICATIONS/275 S. Beverly Dr./Beverly Hills, Cal. 90212

The Time Game

TWO VIEWS OF A PRISON

By **Anthony J. Manocchio**
and **Jimmy Dunn**

with an Introduction and Postscript
by **LaMar T. Empey**

THE TIME GAME has many players, few winners. In this unique double-view of prison life, prisoner Jimmy Dunn and prison psychologist Charles Murray each gives his own view of the same events. Each man approaches the "time game" with different purposes, values, goals. Each plays his part in relation to the other, to the prison system, and to that society beyond the walls —from which each is in his own way cut off.

THE TIME GAME is an important document. What emerges is insight into the **ways** each of these men thinks about and interprets his experience. Their differing, often contradictory, modes of thought never truly come to grips with one another. Despite these differences, the interdependence of prisoner and psychologist as subunits of prison culture becomes clear. Each is a player in a game he cannot win.

The characters and the events are real; all names, with the exception of LaMar T. Empey, are fictitious. Professor Empey, who is Chairman of the Department of Sociology at the University of Southern California, provides an introduction and postscript in which he analyzes the accounts of Dunn and Murray and evaluates them in terms of existing knowledge on the subject.

Along with Professor Empey's interpretations, the personal stories of Dunn and Murray emphasize the need for re-evalua-

(Continued on back flap)